ORIGINAL ORDERS

1/gle
1966
an 1966

THIRD ENDORSEMENT on CG 3dMarDiv Spl0

From: Commanding Officer, Marine Barr   l
         Harbor, Hawaii
To: Sergeant T. K. SALMAN 2009444/0:

Subj: Permanent Change of Station/Leave

1. You reported to this command at 1105, 19 January 1966 for
commencement of leave.

2. Your leave commenced 0900, 18 January 1966. Upon completion of
your leave and no later than 0730, 8 February 1966 you will report
to the Commanding Officer, Marine Barracks, U. S. Naval Base, Pearl
Harbor for duty.

3. Government quarters and messing facilities were available for your
use while at this command.

                                        J. A. BRABHAM
                                        By direction

- -

FOURTH ENDORSEMENT

1. Received these orders at Marine Barracks, U. S. Naval Base, Pearl
Harbor, Hawaii at _____ on _____ 1966.

                    Terry K. Salman

19 - 22 JAN 1966
23 JAN 7 FEB 1966   del

Praise for
WHAT WE GIVE

"Terry Salman, a second-generation Canadian, tells a very personal story of searching for meaning, as a Marine in Vietnam, to finding purpose in random acts of kindness. A worthy read for people who want to change the world."

PIERRE LASSONDE, CM, GOQ, entrepreneur and philanthropist

"*What We Give* reflects a life lived with love, passion, and intensity. Above all, Terry Salman's desire to give back and support those most in need should serve as an inspiration to all. As he illustrates throughout, giving can take many forms, and often the most powerful gift is to help others meet their full potential."

DR. JULIO S.G. MONTANER, OC, OBC, Executive Director and Physician-in-Chief, BC Centre for Excellence in HIV/AIDS

"Reading Terry Salman's words inspires reflection about how we each find our paths, the connections that build our character, and the opportunities to change people's lives through what we give."

CHRISTINA DE CASTELL, Chief Librarian and CEO, Vancouver Public Library

"Terry Salman's fascinating memoir, *What We Give*, starts with him modestly saying that he had the good fortune to have a good life. But more than just that, he is a good man—the man makes the life, and his life was shaped by his extraordinary experiences as a Marine who saw combat in Vietnam, as an investment banker specializing in mining, and as a philanthropist. Whether you are young or just young at heart, reading about his life will bring both pleasure and profit, in particular his wisdom on the importance of friendships, loyalty, and never giving up when the going gets tough."
BILAHARI KAUSIKAN, former Permanent Secretary of the Ministry of Foreign Affairs of Singapore

"Terry Salman speaks of those he has supported through philanthropy with the same reverence he has for fellow Marines and Canadian business titans featured in his impressive military and civilian careers. *What We Give* is a must-read story about military service, personal resilience, the Canadian investment industry, and how a man drew upon all three to give back to his community."
OLIVER THORNE, Executive Director, Veterans Transition Network

"Terry Salman's memoir serves as a poignant reflection on a life lived with purpose. Through his unique life experiences that began in Montreal and took him around the world as a dedicated Marine, a distinguished businessman, and a celebrated philanthropist, Salman's observations on how far corporate culture and inclusion have come are thought-provoking and timely—serving as a reminder of how far society has yet to go to eliminate barriers for a more equitable future."
DARRYL WHITE, CEO, BMO Financial Group

WHAT WE GIVE

TERRY

WHAT WE GIVE

From Marine to Philanthropist:
A Memoir

SALMAN

Some names and identifying details have been
changed to protect the privacy of individuals.

Stanzas from E. Pauline Johnson's "The Song My Paddle Sings"
are quoted in chapter 15, and the full text of John Gillespie Magee's
"High Flight" is quoted in chapter 18.
These works are in the public domain.

All photos courtesy of Terry Salman, except Terry's Marine portrait
(Van Dyck Studio, Montreal); Terry telemark skiing (photo by Rob Tunnock);
Terry with Lauren Bacall, Terry in front of portrait of a Marine, and
Terry in an elevator (all photos by Malcolm Parry).

Cataloguing in publication information is
available from Library and Archives Canada.
ISBN 978-1-77458-187-2 (hardcover)
ISBN 978-1-77458-188-9 (ebook)
ISBN 978-1-77458-287-9 (audiobook)

Page Two
pagetwo.com

Edited by Amanda Lewis and Scott Steedman
Copyedited by Rachel Ironstone
Jacket and interior design by Jennifer Lum
Jacket illustration by Gillian Newland
Printed and bound in Canada by Friesens
Distributed in Canada by Raincoast Books
Distributed in the US and internationally by Macmillan

22 23 24 25 26   5 4 3 2 1

whatwegivebook.com

To Amber, Esme, Naiya, and Hugh,
who love storytelling as much as I do

"We make a living by what we get,
but we make a life by what we give."

WINSTON CHURCHILL

WHAT
WE
GIVE

CONTENTS

AUTHOR'S NOTE

I'VE HAD THE good fortune of having a good life. At first, when a couple of my friends suggested that I write a book, I did not take them seriously. But the lockdowns due to Covid-19 presented a good time to do this, and my wife, Chris, was an early supporter. She felt I had a story that may be worth telling, not to aggrandize what I have done in my life but to hopefully inspire others to do more and give back, especially young people who are looking for direction in their lives.

When I first started to think about writing my memoirs, I went to Jamie Broadhurst of Raincoast Books, whom I had known as a board member of the Vancouver Public Library Foundation. He suggested that I talk to Trena White, one of the two founders of Page Two publishing. So Trena and I sat down over coffee at Thierry, a coffee shop on Alberni Street in Vancouver, and followed that up with several phone calls. She was encouraging about the project, and after meeting with Amanda Lewis, who would become my editor, and the rest of her team, I started to believe that my story could motivate others who come from modest beginnings to reach for higher purposes. My own family had doubts, mostly fearing what I was going to say. But I've always strived for higher goals in my life, and as I've grown older, I've tried to reach for higher moral purposes. These days I feel that we are on this earth for a short time, so we should do what we do best in the limited time allotted us.

What We Give is a way of looking at life that is always in the back of my mind these days. Giving adds purpose to being on this earth. Giving to charity is more about giving time than money, and therefore helping to create a better world. A world that my grandchildren—Amber, Naiya, Esme, and Hugh—will inherit, and where I worry, they may not have as many opportunities as I did.

I've always enjoyed storytelling as a way of getting a message across, a more elegant way of making a point without forcefully telling it so. I hope my story has an impact on you and contributes to how you consider giving more to the world in your own way.

1

MY
FAMILY

I WAS BORN ON May 16, 1942, in Westmount, Quebec, a suburb of Montreal with the highest average income in Canada at the time. But we were anything but rich. My father was a McGill University student, and the hospital where my mother brought me into the world happened to be in Westmount, that is all.

In my early days we lived with my maternal grandmother in Outremont, the suburb where Pierre Elliott Trudeau grew up, while my dad studied mining engineering. Money was tight, and our little family shared the upstairs apartment on 1361 Ducharme Avenue with my uncle Sunny and his wife, Fern.

My father, Tal Salman, had been born in Istanbul, Turkey. His father was a fishery inspector on the Bosporus. Downstairs in my house in Whistler I have a beautiful black-and-white photo of my paternal grandfather, with his grandmother, who raised him after his mother died giving birth to him. She is wearing a hijab over her hair and has deep wrinkles in her face but looks confident and strong. She must have been close to a hundred years old when the photo was taken. Standing with one arm over the old lady's shoulder is Soraya, her great-granddaughter and my father's sister, who graduated from the Sorbonne University in Paris and then went back to Turkey to become a French teacher. All three are smiling happily.

My father was an outstanding student, and in 1939 his high school teacher encouraged him to write an exam sponsored by the Turkish government. The prize was a full scholarship to McGill University, with two conditions: the winner wasn't allowed to drop below third in his class or the benefits would be withdrawn, and they had to return to Turkey to complete their military service after graduation. He wrote the exam and came first in the nation. His elated high school friends and teachers carried my father on their shoulders to his father and announced that he was going to America. His father—who had always told his son he would be a shoeshine boy if he did not study hard—said, "That's impossible, he's too dumb." My dad had that phrase framed on his study wall when I was growing up.

So my father borrowed the equivalent of fifty dollars from his high school teacher and, with his friend Ahmed, boarded the Orient Express at its eastern terminus, Istanbul's Sirkeci Station. This stunning piece of Orientalist architecture near the Golden Horn was opened in 1890 as Turkey's gateway to Europe. The two teenage boys must have been so excited as one of the world's most famous trains carried them through Bucharest, Budapest, Vienna, and Munich, all the way to Paris. The train had to stop at every border town, and the guards would come into the cabin, but after smelling the Turkish sausage they would quickly exit. This did not happen just once but again and again for the whole trip. From Paris, Tal and Ahmed took another train to Calais, where they boarded a ship to New York and then a train to Montreal. I love trains and have taken many exciting train trips in my life; this one I would have loved to have been on.

My mother, Alba May Daniels, grew up in Montreal. Her family didn't have a lot of money to go around, but, judging by pictures from the period, she dressed very smartly and was very attractive. She spoke five languages and sang in a number of choirs around the city. She was a top student at the High School of Montreal, on University Avenue, downtown. The High School was established in 1843 and closed in 1979; coincidentally, it was located right across the street from my father's later office. It had many notable alumni, including actor Christopher Plummer, pianist Oscar Peterson, jewellery store founder Henry Birks, artist Anne Savage, and actress Norma Shearer, who won an Academy Award in 1930 for the rather risqué film *The Divorcee*.

In the early 1930s, my mum was forced to leave high school to take care of her father, who was dying of tuberculosis. Her mother became the family's primary breadwinner with my mother having to work to provide a secondary source of income. Today it's against the law to take a child out of school, but sadly, in those days, there was no social safety net to provide for her or her mother. She had to leave behind her many friends at the High School of Montreal, where she had enjoyed singing, playing the piano, and learning French. I never asked her much about this painful time because it was a difficult subject for her to discuss. She never got over being shortchanged of the education she truly wanted.

My mother met my father at a McGill dance when she was seventeen years old. They were married a year later. My mother was a devoted Christian, so my father, who was a Muslim, converted to Anglicanism, a condition in those days to marry a Christian. I was their first child, followed by my sister a few years later. In total they had six children, five boys and one girl.

I find it hard to talk about my parents because they are no longer with us, but they taught me the best of values. They struggled somewhat as they came from two very different worlds. My father was not the only one in the family who had to convert for love. My mother's father, who was an Italian immigrant and Catholic, also converted to Anglicanism to marry my grandmother, who was English, from Yorkshire. The ceremony was held in St. George's Anglican Church next to Windsor Station. I took a picture of that church last time I visited Montreal; it was winter, but the cold did not prevent me from enjoying the building's beauty. Somewhere in the records of that church is my grandparents' marriage certificate; my daughter Krista found it there some time ago.

In 1943, *The Montreal Star*, a major daily newspaper of that era, printed a picture of my mother, my sister, and me, reporting that we were scheduled to leave for New York and then Europe on the *Gripsholm*, which was famous for being the first diesel-powered ocean liner to cross the Atlantic. After graduating university, my father was returning to Turkey to complete two years of military training, a requirement of his scholarship.

Upon returning to Canada, my father worked for several Canadian mining companies, including Britannia near Vancouver and Noranda in Rouyn-Noranda in Northern Quebec, my favourite place to live as a child. My father was captain at Noranda's high-grade gold and copper Waite-Amulet Mine. We lived in a sprawling house in a remote area fifteen minutes from the mine. It was an amazing place for me. We would listen to Burgess's bedtime stories, and the many characters in his books, like foxes, hares, deer, and bears, were just outside our property. We used to go wild blueberry picking for our breakfast.

One day in Rouyn-Noranda, I noticed, in our garage, a brand-new 1955 Ford Fairlane. It was owned by one of the miners who worked for my dad and who had asked him to protect the car from the harsh winters of Northern Quebec. One day I came home and saw that my father was very sad. The man who owned that beautiful Ford had died in a mining accident. His shirt had been caught by a conveyor belt, and he was pulled to his death.

My father told me many stories like this, like when he worked in Siscoe Gold Mine, near the Cobalt region in Ontario, which produced almost pure, or native, gold. He told me that the ore was so rich and valuable that the miners would often swallow little bits so it would not be picked up by metal detectors when they left their shift. They would later retrieve the gold after a bowel movement. On one of these trips, we toured Canada's first major silver discovery in Cobalt. My father said the sidewalks were made of silver ore because there was so much of it. He told me the story of a blacksmith named LaRose, who threw a hammer at a fox, which dodged away, but the hammer hit silver—that was how the rich silver deposit at Cobalt was discovered. This incident became the subject of a Royal Canadian Mint coin commemorating the discovery of silver in Cobalt, depicting the fox running away from the mine, with an elegant headframe in the background. The original assay was sent to a lab in Ottawa, which said that there was only bismuth in the ore, not silver. The sample was later sent to McGill University mining department for testing, which identified the sample at four thousand ounces per tonne.

That summer we spent in the Cobalt area is one of my fondest teenage memories. While my dad worked at the mine, I water skied on Lac Bass. The water was warm, there were plenty of fish, and the days were long. I did not want to return to Montreal. I also met a girl who liked to water ski, and she taught me how to do it.

My mother did not like mining towns very much—she was a city girl. She longed to return to Montreal, which in those days was Canada's largest city, because she missed its nightlife, architecture, and wonderful choirs, which she often sang in. I loved accompanying her on the nine-hour bus ride from Rouyn-Noranda to Montreal.

I can still remember the excitement of seeing the bus pull up and sitting next to my mother on those long trips back to her hometown.

In 1957, my father applied for a teaching position at McGill. He loved the mining life, but he had no choice—my mother was tired of living in remote mining towns. We eventually moved back to Montreal.

By then I had a sister, Suzan, and a brother, Deniz, who had been born in Izmir on the Turkish Riviera where my father was doing his military service (the Zs in their names are Turkish spellings). My father started lecturing but we did not have much money, so for a while we lived above a horsemeat store, which had a pawn shop below. The apartment was not well heated, so it was very cold during the harsh Montreal winters. My father decided to get his PhD so he could improve his income and stature as a professor. In the years that followed, my parents had three more sons: Kenan, David, and Mark.

My father went on to become a MacDonald Professor of Mining and Metallurgy. When he died in 1979, the Secretary General of the McGill Senate said that the UN said he was "one of the world's leading experts on the ancient art of metal and mineral dressing." While he was at McGill, he travelled the world as a consultant. I always looked forward to his coming home from trips to exotic places like Zambia, when he would give me the sleeping socks they provided passengers on first-class flights in those days. As the university said in their tribute to him on his death, "In his eyes, McGill University could do no wrong. He had come a long way when he took off his old shoes in Turkey and changed into a new pair of shoes as he entered the McGill campus through the Roddick Gates on Sherbrooke Street in Montreal."

My parent were opposites culturally, but not morally. My father revered Atatürk, who believed in the separation of church and state; to quote the Turkish leader, "I have no religion, and at times

I wish all religions at the bottom of the sea. He is a weak ruler who needs religion to uphold his government; it is as if he would catch his people in a trap. My people are going to learn the principles of democracy, the dictates of truth, and the teachings of science." My father also admired Atatürk for his strong support of women's rights, which the Islamic rulers today do not share. Under his leadership, Turkey gave full political rights to women, including the right to vote and be elected, before many European countries, including France, Italy, and Greece.

By the time we moved to 11885 Filion Street, now Rue Filion, my mother and father had six children, and his income was improving as he was now an assistant professor at McGill. Despite his support of Atatürk, my father did not want my mother to work as this was not acceptable in Turkish culture.

It almost seemed like my parents had two families, because of the age difference between we first three children and the later three. My three youngest brothers were still very small when I left home at age twenty. David was the middle child of the three younger boys, and probably the smartest of us all. He was a student in my dad's last graduating class at McGill in mining engineering and went on to complete his MBA at University of Western Ontario. My sister, Suzan, had the most difficult life of us all, not least because she was the only girl among the six of us.

My parents later moved to 59 Winston Circle in Pointe-Claire, a more upscale neighbourhood where prominent businessmen lived, like the president of Tilden Rent-a-Car and the president of the Canadian Pacific Mining subsidiary called Cominco, which is now owned by Teck Resources. I never lived in that house; by then I had already moved to the United States to join the Marine Corps.

As a child I was happy enough, but home life was kind of chaotic. In many ways, I was a normal teenager. It was easy to get around Montreal on streetcars, which I loved and took whenever I could.

One of my favourite streetcars was called Bleury, as it took me down Bleury Street past the tailor shops where my grandfather on my mother's side had worked when he arrived from Naples, Italy, in the early part of the century. His last name was Damiano, which he had to change to Daniels due to the strong anti-Italian feelings during the Mussolini period. I never met him because he died before I was born.

I also loved taking the streetcar to the Montreal Forum, where the Canadiens played. I enjoyed looking around the Forum and Tupper Street, where we used to live when I was the only child and my father was a McGill student. Sometimes I would go to the old Delorimier Stadium, where Jackie Robinson had played baseball for the Montreal Royals. My friends and I also sometimes put small silver bullets on the streetcar tracks, which sounded like firecrackers when they exploded.

My fondest memory of my father is from Saint Patrick's Day, 1955. It was the night of the Richard Riot, one of the most important games in National Hockey League history. Four days earlier, I had listened to the commentator from the Boston Garden on my shortwave radio as he described the violent scenes during a game between the Montreal Canadiens and the Boston Bruins. A linesman, Cliff Thompson, grabbed the Montreal star Maurice Richard, which allowed the Boston defenseman Hal Laycoe to punch Richard again and again in the head. Richard broke free, decked the linesman, and then proceeded to hit Laycoe in the head with a hockey stick. A few days later, Richard was suspended for the rest of the NHL season and the playoffs, which ultimately made him forfeit the chance of winning the Art Ross Trophy (for topping the league in points scored). The suspension outraged the Québécois, who thought he was being unfairly punished for being French.

Somehow, my father got two tickets for the next Canadiens game, against the Detroit Red Wings. We were sitting in the prime red seats in the Forum looking at Clarence Campbell, the president of the NHL. By the time the second period came around, he was being pelted by fans with eggs and all sorts of debris. Then came the smoke bombs, to the point where you could barely see players on the ice. The Montreal fire marshal closed the Forum and kicked everyone out. As we made our way through the smoke out of the building onto Sainte-Catherine Street, we saw police cars turned over and vandalized shops. It was not common for a thirteen-year-old boy to hold his father's hand, but I did that night. We never went to another hockey game together after that.

I worked at the golf course where I learned how to play golf right-handed, even though I was left-handed; they did not have any left-handed clubs. I practised with other caddies by turning up at six thirty in the morning before the club members started to arrive. On summer evenings my friends and I often played ball hockey until it was dark. When it got too cold and snow began to fall in the late fall or early winter, we started playing ice hockey in an open outdoor rink not far from our house. I have the fondest memories of those games, which I never wanted to end. Even as the temperature dropped in the middle of winter, playing hockey was hard to pass up.

In football season, my father often took me to watch McGill football games, because he was entitled to free tickets as a professor. I loved the game and was inspired to join my high school team; I had the speed back then to play tailback, sometimes as a ball carrier. I remember the school field high above the city, up near Mount Royal. I can still recall the smell of freshly cut grass in the fall during our practice.

Unfortunately, academics were not my forte, and my grades kept dropping throughout high school. I found many activities to be much more interesting than studying. I had several motorcycles and spent a lot of time riding them and engaging in other pastimes that were not particularly productive. I hung around with my friends, playing hockey and occasionally rolling out one of my friends' father's car for a midnight joy ride. Eventually we got caught and ended up in the police station. It was hard to look my father in the eyes when he came to collect me.

2

THE MARINES ARE LOOKING FOR A FEW GOOD MEN

I JOINED THE UNITED States Marine Corps on June 18, 1962. I remember my father driving me to the recruiting centre in Plattsburgh, New York, from Montreal. The road to Plattsburgh is flat and picturesque, down Highway 15 and I-87 south, past the farming community of Saint-Jean-sur-Richelieu and the beautiful town of Napierville.

I do not remember much about the drive except that I was very quiet. My mother refused to come along because she was really opposed to me joining the Marines. I was nervous and sad at the same time, and I kept wondering if I would ever see my father or my mother again. I was starting to miss them already. I thought about changing my mind, but I had already made my decision. I have often wondered how my father felt after dropping me off. Was he sad too?

My father's Turkish government scholarship to McGill had set a high bar for all of us. I joined the Marines to try to prove to him that I could do something to make him proud and overcome my poor grades and performance in high school. By then I had failed at a number of high schools, including one boarding school, and I knew it was nothing to be proud of. In Montreal schools back then, bad boys like me would have to stand in the front of the class and put out our open hands to be strapped by the teacher until our fingers were blue. Little did I know that this barbaric practice would be repeated by a drill instructor in boot camp in the Marines. John Steinbeck's greatest belief was in the ability of people to improve their own condition, and I now realize that's what I was trying to do, though I was too young to see it that way at the time.

The Marines recruiter looked very polished in his blue dress pants with the red vertical stripe depicting the bloody loss of 138 Marines at the Battle of Chapultepec during the Mexican–American War of 1847. Behind his desk I noticed a picture of President John F. Kennedy over a plaque saying he was the commander-in-chief. As a twenty-year-old, I was very impressed with President Kennedy, who would make a lasting impression on me during my new life in the United States.

I signed up on the spot. In the early spring of 1962, I was going nowhere. My grades in high school were dropping, and the most notable thing I had done for months was buy a Triumph Bonneville motorcycle from a man who had hit a cow while riding it on the Saint-Lazare highway. Thanks to my uncle Willy, who was a welder, we were able to restore the frame. I purchased a new front wheel and now had an almost-new motorcycle. I proceeded to spend that spring getting enough speeding tickets to plaster my bedroom wall, from a police officer who would wait for me to leave my house every day. One day in early spring, I hit black ice on the Victoria Bridge while crossing the St. Lawrence River, narrowly missing death; I spun around through several lanes without hearing or hitting a car. Somehow, I was able to pick up the bike and ride home, albeit slowly. How I loved that Triumph Bonneville! It could easily hit a hundred miles per hour without my remotely feeling like I was going that fast. Riding that bike was an adrenaline rush, a memorable experience that was short-lived.

I could afford the bike because I had landed a bartending job at the bar on the roof of the Queen Elizabeth Hotel, a grand establishment now owned by Fairmont, in the heart of downtown Montreal. I operated a martini wagon and wore a button-down white-and-red-striped jacket with a black bowtie. My most notable guest was the actress Angie Dickinson, who was thirty years old and very attractive. I got sick with jaundice while working there; we washed the glasses by hand in the bar, so I must have picked up an infection at work. The doctor gave me some antibiotics and made me stay home until I recovered. I couldn't wait to get back to the martini wagon—I loved working there and had learned how to make perfect martinis to order: Beefeater Gin with a twist, martinis with a splash of vermouth. I ran the whole process, and the martini business was mine.

Martini wagon aside, my life was stalled in neutral, and I was anxious to find a more glamorous career path. I considered joining the Canadian Army, but then I heard that they were mainly peacekeepers, which didn't inspire me. Then I read about the Marines and their claim to be "the finest fighting force in the world." That impressed me. So did the sight of their dress blues. The recruiter made me feel special, though he told me that the Marines only took a few applicants. I had read the book *Battle Cry* by Leon Uris and was fascinated by the hero, Danny, who joins the Marines at seventeen by lying about his age. Reading the story of how Danny and a ragtag group of other Marines come together as a team, and the attractive women they fall in love with in New Zealand, made me want to join up right away. To this day I am fascinated with the city of Wellington in New Zealand, where the 3rd Marine Division was stationed prior to attacking Guadalcanal in World War II.

I have never been there, but I've always wanted to go. The lives of the enlisted characters in *Battle Cry* were raw, and I dreamed of living a life like theirs.

The recruiter continued to charm me with the stories of a life of travel and exotic places. He went on to tell me that the Marines had good experiences with Canadian recruits. I found out shortly thereafter that Marines are stationed in every US embassy abroad— Paris, Rome, Bermuda—and on every major ship of the US Navy. It was hard not to romanticize life as a Marine with all those duty stations offered.

As we drove to Plattsburgh, I had already been worrying that I might never return to Montreal, being somewhat fatalistic about where the Marines would take me. After I signed up, I was given a one-way ticket on a commercial flight to Beaufort, South Carolina. It was the first time I'd ever been on a plane. I can still remember the attractive young flight attendants telling me I would regret this trip and putting the fear of God into me after I told them I was joining the Marines. They said I would need a few drinks and proceeded to serve them to me, on the house. Upon landing, I was met by yelling and screaming instructors. We were herded off, one by one, and shoved into buses bound for Parris Island, the Marine Corps Recruit Depot in South Carolina.

Parris Island was surrounded by swamp and quicksand. On April 5, 1956, just six years before I arrived, Sergeant Matthew McKeon had forced a group of recruits to do a night march through the backwaters of the island in an effort to restore flagging discipline. An unexpectedly strong tidal current in Ribbon Creek swept over the recruits, and six of them drowned.

It is ten miles from Beaufort to PI, and the bus ride only took twenty minutes, but it seemed like an eternity. As we approached the base, I saw a sign that read "Marine Corps Recruit Depot, SC" and felt a sense of fear and anxiety. It was night and the air was warm. I could see the MPs (military policemen) in the distance as the bus made its way through the iron gates. Today if you were to visit PI, you would see yellow footprints on the pavement where the recruits line up and a big silver sign atop the door or "hatch." It reads, "Through these portals pass prospects for America's finest fighting force."

From the moment you arrive at the recruit depot, your ass belongs to the Marines. When we got off the bus, every single civilian item was stripped from us and shipped home. As every recruit on PI knows, you are not a Marine until you graduate at the end of thirteen weeks of boot camp. Before that, you'd be called a turd, a maggot, a slime bucket, and a packet of many other names, especially if you were Canadian. The drill instructors often screamed at me, "What are you doing in *my* Marine Corps?" They would also make me sing "God Save the Queen" butt-naked and upside down. If you're a foreigner, you stand out and are sure to take some verbal abuse or be ordered to do a large number of push-ups or sit-ups or run a mile or so in combat gear. The Marines make their recruits face the greatest challenges during the formal thirteen-week program, most of which are never shared with anyone. This code of silence is just the way it is—man to man, rarely written down. Like the French Foreign Legion, the United States Marine Corps doesn't care where you're from—only whether you have what it takes to be a Marine.

PI is not a forgiving place. The swamp, the quicksand, the mosquitos, and the intense heat were often too much to bear. As recruits we all hoped for a red-flag day, when the drill instructors could not march us outside. But they only made it worse for us on those days by making us march with our footlockers on our shoulders in the barracks, away from others' watch.

Marine Corps boot camp was the hardest thing I have ever experienced in my life. For thirteen weeks, I went through more physically and mentally demanding conditions than I had ever thought possible. From 0400 hours until lights-out in the evening (around 2000h), we were put through extensive physical activities such as running and swimming, not to mention hours of handbook course work. We were also trained in judo, pugil stick fighting, and bayonet fighting.

Marines are first and foremost riflemen, and every Marine graduate, unlike recruits in every other service, must qualify firing an M14 at 200, 300, and 500 yards, without a scope and with no part of the rifle's butt touching the ground. The Marine doctrine, the Rifleman's Creed, states:

This is my rifle. There are many like it, but this one is mine. It is my life. I must master it as I must master my life. Without me, my rifle is useless. Without my rifle, I am useless. I must fire my rifle true. I must shoot straighter than the enemy who is trying to kill me. I must shoot him before he shoots me. I will. My rifle and I know that what counts in war is not the rounds we fire, the noise of our burst, or the smoke we make. We know that it is the hits that count. We will hit.

My rifle is human, even as I am human, because it is my life. Thus, I will learn it as a brother. I will learn its weaknesses, its strengths, its parts, its accessories, its sights, and its barrel. I will keep my rifle clean and ready, even as I am clean and ready. We will become part of each other.

Before God I swear this creed. My rifle and I are the defenders of my country. We are the masters of our enemy. We are the saviors of my life.

So be it, until victory is America's and there is no enemy.

This was the official version, written by Major General William H. Rupertus in 1942. There is another version that we sang privately in the barracks: "This is my rifle. This is my gun," pointing at one's penis. "This one's for fighting. This one's for fun."

At boot camp, recruits are mentally and physically broken down before being rebuilt to become US Marines. At PI, recruits are kept away from the watchful eyes of politicians and family, and are solely at the mercy of the drill instructors. About 20 percent of them do not graduate in their platoon and are sent away to receive additional training.

I had no time to make friends and spent thirteen weeks almost entirely silent, except after lights-out. Most of the communication happened between the drill instructors and me. Mosquitos were everywhere, and anyone who attempted to swat them would be reprimanded by the drill instructors: "Why are you killing my mosquitos, you turd?" We all feared that we would not graduate after thirteen weeks and would be left behind in the motivational platoon. Or, even worse, be given a dishonourable discharge, a bad conduct discharge, or a medical discharge, any one of which would have a negative impact even on civilian life.

Of all the training in PI, the toughest part was probably crawling under barbed wire in full combat uniforms while bullets, which we never knew were real or not, were sprayed across the field atop our heads. My biggest fear, however, was jumping out of a helicopter on a rope—an exercise I tried to get out of by going to the sick bay. Once in the helicopter, fear set in as I looked down. I had to remember to wrap the rope over the top of one of my boots and press down on the other boot while keeping a strong grip overhead.

Swimming the full length of a pool with all my combat gear on was the closest I've come to drowning. The drill instructor paid little attention to how much water I was taking in. His only remark was how poorly I could swim despite coming from Canada, where there is plenty of water. I was told that if you fail swimming in the Marine Corps, you're done, so I treaded water until my arms and legs ached while the DI paced the length of the pool deck.

But boot camp was so much more than any one thing—it was intense training every hour of every day of your waking life. One day we'd be running through an obstacle course learning how to get our asses through but also to help other Marines along the way if they were struggling. The next day we had to walk up to twenty miles a day with a full pack, or learn judo or pugil stick fighting, or a whole bunch of other things that are not in the manual. You burned five thousand calories a day and the training hadn't been shortened for the Vietnam War, as it would be later.

One of my drill instructors, Sergeant Wilson, came from Windsor, Ontario. He was a kind man. But being a Canadian subjected me to a lot of verbal abuse. One DI occasionally hit me with a riding crop when the other recruits were not watching. I guessed that he was testing me, for some reason. A few years later when I was leaving Vietnam, I saw him arriving for his tour of duty—he was still a corporal as he had been back then on PI, and I was now his superior, having been promoted to sergeant.

One day, prior to the end of boot camp, the DI pointed at me in the back row and told me that I was in charge of the platoon, and to march the platoon to "chow," Marine corps nomenclature for "lunch." This was the first time I had ever been in charge of anybody, a first leadership role that I would never forget. The Marine Corps makes leaders out of nobodies, and for some strange reason, I was able to drill this platoon with all the proper cadence and commands that I had learned over the preceding thirteen weeks on Parris Island: "Left, right, left, right, get in step, recruits!"

When I look back now, I am grateful to the recruiter in Plattsburg who signed me up. Of the many men he recruited, I was one of the very few Canadians. People say that PI is one of the cradles of the Marine Corps. Of all the honours I've had in my life, nothing was as important as graduating as a Marine in early October of 1962. My parents and three of my brothers, David, Kenan, and Mark, attended my graduation ceremony. That fall on PI changed my life forever. I had followed the path of all the other Marines who had come before me, an honour few had the opportunity to achieve.

As I left Parris Island for the last time, I saw again the sign that read, "Marine Corps Recruit Depot, SC." The MPs' sharp salute made us all teary-eyed and gave us a sense of pride as Marines. I would later visit the other recruit depot in San Diego when I was stationed in California. It was always under the watchful eye of politicians, Hollywood types, and concerned parents, so different from remote and isolated PI. My drill instructor used to say, "We are surrounded by quicksand, and there's no way out unless you become a US Marine."

A sense of sadness came over me as we rode the bus north. From Beaufort, the Greyhound headed to Jacksonville, North Carolina, before arriving at Camp Lejeune, one of the Marine Corps' largest bases. I reported to 2nd Battalion, 6th Marines, one of only two units in the Corps to wear the French fourragère, a regimental distinction instituted by Napoleon and bestowed upon them after the Battle of Belleau Wood in World War I. In Marine Corps history, this is one of the most significant battles, at which the American forces suffered devastating casualties. The French awarded the regiment the Croix de Guerre, to be worn on the left shoulder. I found myself wondering why I had been selected to join this distinguished unit. To quote Leon Uris in *Battle Cry*, "the regiment was one of those proud outfits that has been settling wars for decades, where we stop the Hun dead in its tracks. For doing so, the French decorated us with a fancy braid called the Fourragère."

Camp Lejeune is a sprawling base with fourteen miles of beach for amphibious assault training. Finally, I had a sense of freedom. After thirteen weeks of non-stop training, I also had the occasional day off—one time I even received a ninety-six-hour pass, which was extremely rare. Corporal Franklin—a handsome fellow some said looked like Clark Gable—two other Marines, and I headed to New Jersey, where I encountered one of the scariest experiences of my life.

As we entered a dark road near Charlottesville, Virginia, we were confronted by a group of people in white hoods and torches gathered around a fire. As one of the men approached us, our driver screamed, "Holy shit! These are the Ku Klux Klan," and told us to bury our fellow African American Marine under our feet and cover him with a blanket. The hooded man held up his torch and scanned our car. After a very tense pause, he waved us on.

This was my first encounter with racial intolerance in the United States. To say I was scared would be an understatement; I was convinced that if they had found our Black Marine friend, they would have hanged him. We were not in our uniforms, but I don't believe that would have made a difference. Shaken, we continued our drive to New Jersey. We made several trips to the state that summer, and fortunately we never saw the KKK again. But race came up again and again in the Marines, and I just didn't understand it. One time I was sitting on a bus when I heard the driver tell a fellow Marine in uniform to go to the back of the bus. I asked him why, to which he responded, "That's the way it is in the South, Marine." A few minutes earlier, I had witnessed washrooms that said "Colored," which felt strange, but in the South in the sixties, you didn't ask too many questions. It felt safer at times to be on the base.

In the next five months at Camp Lejeune, we learned to be the best battle-trained Marines possible. I was given MOS (military occupational specialty) training on 81mm mortars, a medium-distance weapon attached to a rifle company in the 6th Marines. Our time at Camp Lejeune was short-lived, however, as we boarded the USS *Francis Marion* for duty with the US 6th Fleet in the Mediterranean in March of 1963.

Corporal Franklin and I were about to have the time of our lives. It was Camelot. We were not the ugly Americans that everyone wanted to see us as. Every port of call had a welcoming party. Best of all, Cpl Franklin was with the 6th Marines military police, so shore leave suddenly became an opportunity to party late into the night. We were twenty years old, and we were about to visit Genoa, Barcelona, Palermo, Nice on the French Riviera, and Naples, as sort of goodwill ambassadors for the United States. Large crowds greeted us, among them many young and attractive girls. People would say, "Hi Marine, do you have a Zippo light and jeans?" Between visits to these ports, we practised war games, such as maneuvers on long marches in Sardinia. The miles would go by, and we couldn't wait to camp for the night or return to the ship to shower, but not before we had a cold beer on shore. The ship always had plenty of beer but only for shore leave. We were not allowed to drink on the ship.

We also practised maneuvers with the Turkish army, which the most famous Marine Chesty Puller had called the best troops in the Korean War. We were given the example of when a Turkish platoon was captured by the Chinese. They were interrogated as prisoners: "Who's in charge here?" And every single Turkish soldier replied, "I am." When I asked the Turkish commander we were training with how to keep an enemy prisoner down, he showed me the steel heel on his boot and how he would put that on the captive's face.

One of my favourite ports of call was Barcelona, with its wide boulevards and outdoor cafés. One of our Marine friends was married to a Spanish girl, who told us where to go and where to eat.

Naples is where my grandfather on my mother's side came from. He immigrated to North America and worked as a tailor on Bleury Street. Palermo and Sicily were friendly places where many locals invited us into their homes to share food and wine. We learned that fall to climb a rope ladder to board the ship from a Mike Boat (LCM-8), an exercise made more difficult in the rough seas. The idea was for several Marines to keep the net tight while I climbed up to the ship in full combat gear.

Cannes, France, was a special place in the sixties, with great food and beautiful women, many topless, sunbathing on some of the best beaches in the Mediterranean. We were welcomed by many beautiful people, who loved to party and invited us to join. The young women especially liked the young Marines. On May 9, we managed to enjoy the Cannes Film Festival, or at least one aspect of it—the many parties that surrounded it and would go on until May 23. One mother tried to set up her beautiful daughter with my friend Cpl Franklin.

This place was hard to leave, and sometimes men got left behind. Going AWOL (absent without leave, or permission) is not a good position to be in in the Marines as it has severe penalties. Occasionally, we also had a man overboard, and never saw him again.

Unfortunately, all good things must come to an end, and as summer ended, we headed back to the US. The four-day return sail was brutal; the North Atlantic can be very rough in mid-October. The Marines found ways to keep us busy, painting the ship, polishing the brass, and learning how to transfer food from one ship to another. Of course, we all had guard duty, which was unbearable as seawater sprayed into our faces as the ship plowed its way through giant swells and cold rain. At one point I looked down and saw four sailors playing cards underneath the hatch. We played a lot of cards, and some of us were very good—we often bet a week's salary or more.

The six months in the 6th Marines were some of the best times of my life. The summer of 1963 was going to be hard to beat. Returning to Camp Lejeune was a huge letdown after the French Riviera.

—

THEY SAY everyone remembers where they were when they heard the news. I was in a taxi in Washington, DC, in uniform, when I heard Walter Cronkite on the radio announcing that President Kennedy had just been killed. He was my hero, and one of the reasons I had joined the Marines. I stumbled out of the taxi in disbelief.

When I read the story in the newspaper and saw that Lee Harvey Oswald, the man who had killed President Kennedy, was a Marine, one of the saddest days of my life felt even sadder. From a window eighty-eight yards away, he had fired his mail-order Italian rifle at the president. Like Oswald, I had qualified as a Marine with an M-14 rifle to get my sharp-shooting badge; I had scored 219, one point below an expert score of 220. I would go on to use the same semiautomatic rifle in the Vietnam War, the ones Marines still use today for ceremonial occasions; the silent US Marine Corps drill team, for instance, uses M-14s with linseed-polished wood handles. All this knowledge made November 22, 1963, a sad day for all Marines.

I spent that Christmas with a girl I was dating in Fairlawn, New Jersey, which the *New York Times* called "an unpretentious place that smelled like cookies." I met Pat Marton through Corporal Franklin's girlfriend. She was a sweet twenty-year-old from a wonderful Italian family. She was easy to get along with, and I so looked forward to seeing her on those long trips from North Carolina. We enjoyed a number of good times together, including that Christmas of 1963, and were even engaged briefly. But I broke off our engagement because I just couldn't make a commitment. I was twenty years old, and she was my first love. I told her to keep her engagement ring.

Sadly, I never saw Pat again. I left the East Coast a few months later, my future uncertain. I was being shipped westward into the unknown. Before I left, I managed to return to Montreal to see my family. Then I headed for California, leaving most of my best friends and my family behind and fearing I would never see them again.

I left the 6th Marines and was transferred to another famous Marine unit, 1st Battalion, 4th Marines, known as the China Marines because of their duty in Shanghai prior to the Japanese occupation in World War II. Their motto reads, "Whatever it takes." The unit was based in Kaneohe Bay on the island of Oahu in Hawaii, the first place the Japanese strike force had attacked on the way to Pearl Harbor. But before going there we first spent a few months in Camp Pendleton, a large Marine Corps base in Southern California.

California in the sixties was a beautiful place, with the best roads in America. Camp Pendleton is near the small town of Oceanside, a short drive down Route 66 along the Southern California coast to San Diego, a thriving city with a population of around 800,000 at that time. My stay in California was wonderful, however brief it was—light traffic, small population, great beaches, and great climate.

Shortly, we boarded a ship to Honolulu. When we arrived in Pearl Harbor, we were greeted by girls dancing the hula. I don't think the Navy arranged this reception; it was just a Hawaiian custom of greeting guests.

It was a special time to live in Hawaii, just after statehood, when not many people had come from the mainland to visit or live—a time before jumbo jets and mass tourism. Hawaiian culture was everywhere; we often listened to Don Ho performing evening shows in the International Market Place on Kalakaua Avenue, the main street in Waikiki. In those days, Kalakaua Avenue was a two-way street, and you could see Waikiki Beach from both sides. Duke Kahanamoku, a local surfing legend and Olympic swimming champion, often parked his bright red Rolls Royce on the street with its familiar Hawaii licence plate that read "DUKE." There was a soda fountain on the beach where you could have an ice-cream soda, sit on a swivel chair, and watch the surfers riding waves off in the distance. The University of Hawaii had the largest summer school in the US, so there was no shortage of girls for the 4th Marines. One Marine I knew was busted three times and sent to the brig for overstaying his leave and going AWOL in Waikiki.

Our base, Kaneohe Bay, was just sixteen miles down the scenic Pali Highway from Fort DeRussy in the heart of Waikiki, where you could enjoy cheap drinks in the NCO (non-commissioned officer) club. The base is still there, and still occupied by the US Army, probably making it the military's most expensive real estate per square foot in the country.

The nightlife in Waikiki was probably the best anywhere. The nights we spent there at the beach went by so quickly. I had a friend in the Corps who joined the Marines on the condition that his parents, who were wealthy, give him a Porsche and an apartment in Waikiki. From the day I met him, I didn't have to take a kamikaze taxi anymore. My friend often took us at top speed down the Pali Highway, to the point where I felt like I was being ejected from the passenger seat. The highway was the most dangerous one on the islands, rising from sea level to twelve hundred feet with major switchbacks that seemed to never end. My friend assured me that his new Porsche was made for this road, and we were on a mission every day: we had to be back at the base by 6 a.m. I can still remember the Marine MP at the gate looking at his watch as we approached the gate at 5:54 a.m. or so.

A Marine's salary didn't take us very far in Waikiki, so it didn't take us long to run out of money. I had another friend, Corporal Baron, who was a pool shark, so to augment our income, with great risk, we played pool for money. Snooker was Cpl Baron's specialty, but rules of pool in this kind of place meant that you had to declare your position as pool shark, which he never did. I was always nervously watching him wrap up the table and eager to leave as the room was often filled with heavily built Samoans.

The Vietnam War was just around the corner, but we didn't know that. Cpl Baron and I were good friends, and we had a lot of fun together in Hawaii. The last time I saw him, he was in the back of a truck in Vietnam. Everyone on that truck was going home; their tour of duty was ending. All of them were badly wounded and had been bandaged up by the Navy Corpsmen, revered by the Marines. I visited Cpl Baron in a temporary jungle hospital the Navy had put together, where the wounded were treated before being sent home. His leg was bandaged as he had somehow been hit by one of our own grenades. He was not particularly looking forward to going home. He loved the Marine life. I said "Goodbye, buddy" as the helicopter he'd been loaded into lifted off to take him to the hospital ship anchored in the South China Sea. I remember tearing up as I lost sight of the helicopter in the heat.

I'm sad to say that I never saw Cpl Baron again. Later, I'm sure he and all the men he lay with in that hospital suffered intangible mental conditions; this was before people talked about mental illness or PTSD. Such was the war in Vietnam in the sixties. Friends and strangers were wounded, their lives forever damaged by war. Most of us did not understand the long-term impact.

But I'm getting ahead of myself. The 1st Battalion, 4th Marines, were a storied outfit who would earn two Medals of Honor in Vietnam, and I had wonderful friends there while it lasted. In those days, this Marine Corps unit was small, topped at eight hundred men, so we had the best training for the longest period. We were professional soldiers and the best fighting men America had.

I had a few good friends and commanders then. Two of the most inspirational were Second Lieutenant Kent Valley and Corporal Patrick.

Second Lieutenant Kent Valley was a platoon commander and a polished Marine who gave me the best conduct and proficiency score I ever received. He scored me five out of five, which he then reduced to 4.9 because the commanding officer said, "No one is that perfect." I admired 2nd Lt Valley to no end. We were friends and went to Vietnam together.

Rarely do magazine articles hit me personally. But that is exactly what happened when my wife, Chris, gave me the August 2021 issue of *Leatherneck*, one of the two Marine Corps magazines. I opened it up and read "Land of the Free" by Sara W. Bock, one of the featured articles of the month. The article points out that *Leatherneck* was founded by Kent Valley and two of his friends. I learned that their charity, Land of the Free, has donated more than $15 million to military-related causes.

Second Lieutenant Kent Valley supported me in many ways, not the least of which was promoting me to corporal and likely supported my promotion later to sergeant. He had a marked impact in my life as a role model of what a Marine should be, and I tried to live up to his confidence in me for the rest of my time in the Marine Corps. The conduct and proficiency marks he gave me were the highest possible and I always tried to fulfill his expectations for me. In my letters to my wife, Ronna, from Vietnam I often mentioned 2nd Lt Valley, so in a way his manner of giving back to me encouraged me to consciously give back to others. I learned from the *Leatherneck* article that he is now a senior officer of one of the largest land companies in the US.

Corporal Patrick was one of the most gung-ho Marines I've ever met: strong, good-looking, "squared away" as the Marines say. I admired him and wanted to be like him. He did everything well and inspired me to push myself to a new level of proficiency.

Corporal Patrick fell in love in 1964 with a girl whose family put her up in a fancy hotel in Waikiki. She was a beautiful girl and not the kind most Marines would meet—she had lovely brown hair and was properly raised. Cpl Patrick told me she was a virgin. Her parents were well-off and had sent her to Hawaii on a trip to celebrate her university graduation. Months later, when we were suddenly shipped to Vietnam, I lost touch with him, and I always wondered if he had married that girl.

Corporal Patrick taught me to be the best Marine I could be. I will always remember him in his starched uniform shirt, sleeves creased precisely through his chevrons. His belt was always centred where his shirt met the trousers, which were always perfectly creased.

3

THE CALM
BEFORE
THE STORM

IT WAS EASY to relax into Waikiki's sensual days and evenings. We were Marines, and there were many things to do, like surf, sunbathe, and play handball at a court on the beach at Fort DeRussy. Day turns to night, and Michener's Hawaii was hard to leave. The warm trade winds ensured that you were never too hot or too cool.

Singers in the open-air bars sang soft Hawaiian tunes that have passed the test of time—the songs never got old, though the singers did. Don Ho was the star of the sixties, so were Nat King Cole and Kui Lee. Kui's teacher always said that when Kui was not in school, he knew the surf was up. The Marines fell in love easily in Hawaii. The conditions were perfect for it, and the space was just right for two people.

I met Ronna outside the Elizabeth Arden salon on Kalakaua Avenue in the summer of 1964. It was a couple blocks away from the International Market Place, a large open-air market in the centre of Waikiki, and across the street from the Copper Kitchen, a local restaurant. I approached her and introduced myself. I must have surprised her somewhat, especially with my traditional

Marine Corps haircut, which is to say, hardly any hair. I asked her if I could wait for her to talk to her after her visit to the salon. I don't recall what I did while I was waiting, but I probably took a walk along Waikiki Beach.

After that, I saw Ronna every chance I could. We spent weekends enjoying Waikiki and all the beaches in Honolulu; to this day, Honolulu is the only city where I do not have to use a GPS.

Training in those days before we were shipped to Vietnam was tough, as the Marines were trying to make the 1st Battalion, 4th Marines, a fighting force fit for the battlegrounds of Vietnam. Training included hiking on every island of Hawaii, except Ni'ihau. I remember being very seasick off the coast of Maui and praying that I would get off the ship soon.

When I returned from Vietnam, Ronna and I rented our first apartment in Waikiki on Kuhio Avenue, a couple blocks away from the legendary Sheraton Moana, now the Moana Surfrider Westin, where the big banyan tree still stands in the middle of the hotel facing Waikiki Beach. Stores that don't exist anymore dotted Kalakaua Avenue: Liberty House, Copper Kitchen, Canlis, and Dorothea's shop, which was owned by a friend of my future mother-in-law, Ruth. Ronna introduced me to her and to her stepdad, John Wade, who were wonderfully engaging people and welcomed me into their home.

Ronna was easy to get along with. She was willing to try so many different things. We often sipped the cheap Mai Tais or piña coladas on offer at the NCO club at Fort DeRussy and spent sensual evenings at the wonderful restaurants by the beach and walking along the coast afterwards. It was a sharp contrast to the pool halls and bars of downtown Honolulu that Cpl Baron and I had spent our evenings in before I met Ronna. The hotel street area of Honolulu reminded me of the scenes in *From Here to Eternity* when

Private Prewitt fell in love with Alma at the New Congress Club on River Street; Prewitt was shot dead by MPs in Fort DeRussy Beach Park, where Ronna and I often walked. Today the area has another pool hall called Velvet Touch Billiards, which according to reviewers "has a ghetto-ass location."

I continued to train and live at the base in Kaneohe. We kept beach towels and bathing suits in Ronna's car in preparation of a day off. The H-1 freeway hadn't been built back then, but there was little traffic and driving around the island provided endless adventures.

Most people don't realize that the island of Oahu has around 125 beaches. We made sure to swim and surf as many of them as possible. The North Shore beaches have huge waves in fall and winter, which die off in the summer. My favourite was Pipeline with its giant curling waves that roll up high from the sea and propel surfers into deep tubes before crashing into a foaming mass right by the shore. I was not a good enough surfer to tackle those famous waves, but I sure enjoyed watching others do it.

We were in love, and every hour and day mattered as Vietnam was on everybody's mind. We both knew that my time on Oahu was limited. I knew I'd be leaving soon when the Marines told me my battalion was no longer officially based out of Kaneohe Bay; I now had a San Francisco address: 1st Batt 4th Marines 3rd Div FMF, FPO SAN FRANCISCO, California, USA 96601. This is the Marine Corps' way of allowing us to receive mail while keeping our true location secret.

Ronna and I decided to get married at St. Andrew's Cathedral in Honolulu, a famous church that Queen Emma had built during the period Hawaii was under a monarchy. This stunning French Gothic–style cathedral is illuminated by large westward-facing windows that bathe parishioners in golden Hawaiian sunlight, including a stained-glass window with a large standing image of

Christ. During the monarchy period, those opposed to statehood sat on the right-side pews while those in favour sat on the left. To this day, there are paintings on the walls of the kings and queens of Hawaii. There was no time to plan a big wedding, so we were officiated by Dean Morriet of the cathedral, a survivor of the Bataan Death March (a forcible transfer by the Imperial Japanese Army during WWII).

During the short period after our wedding, we did what most couples did before we went to war. We made the best of the small things and moments—beach walks, evenings out, family barbecues. Ronna's family were successful, well-known people who held large social gatherings. John Wade, her stepfather, was like a real father figure to her, an iconic man who owned a large distributor of magazines in California. At one point, he also owned the second-largest ranch in Canada; he used to say, "It would almost take a full day to drive the length of the property." He had sold the ranch to the Mormon Church and moved to Hawaii to build his magazine distribution business. When the Mormon Church asked him his preferred method of payment for the transaction, he told them cash. So church officials flew up to the ranch with a million dollars in a suitcase.

Ronna's stepfather had met Ronna's mother, Ruth, at the Hotel Vancouver, where she worked at the front desk. To downplay his wealth while they were dating, he would pick her up at the hotel in an old pickup truck, a far cry from the Cadillac he drove in Hawaii with the custom licence plate, "WADE." His two children, Ruth's stepchildren, lived in Hawaii. The Wades were family to me in the months before I left Pearl Harbor.

Ronna continued to live with her parents while I lived at the base at Kaneohe Bay. In the early spring of 1965, I received orders to report to the USS *Valley Forge*. I had been on two-year-duty in Hawaii. This brief Camelot period was about to end.

After I packed up my belongings that day, Ronna drove me to Pearl Harbor along with a friend of mine, Private Treadway, who I never saw again (in those days before the internet, it was difficult to keep in touch with people, and as Marines, we never knew where we would be next). The *Valley Forge*, my new home, was an LPH, or "landing platform helicopter," a US Navy aircraft carrier with helicopters and a combat infantry unit of the US Marine Corps stationed aboard. The ship was three football fields long and an imposing sight from the deck to a twenty-year-old. Named after the spot where George Washington camped his Continental Army, it had been converted from an aircraft carrier to a helicopter carrier for the Vietnam War. It was an amphibious assault ship that carried over 3,500 sailors and Marines, launching Marines into battle on UH-1 helicopters, nicknamed "Hueys." I remember clearly climbing onto the ship the first time and saluting proudly to the officers on deck while saying, "Corporal Salman requests permission to come onboard, sir." No civilians of any type were allowed on the ship, including Ronna.

We set sail for Yokohama, the second-largest city in Japan, to enjoy some R&R (rest and relaxation). Onboard the ship, we engaged in multiple tasks, including extensive workouts, class training, and mundane duties like cleaning and polishing the brass. Some of us played instruments to entertain each other, and there were movies we could watch in the ship's theatre.

Our bunks were stacked in rows. I was a corporal, so I had a little more room. But if you had to go to the head to use the washroom, you almost had to step on your fellow Marines below you. On the way to Yokohama, we gambled away our eighty-dollar-a-month salaries, wrote letters home, and practised loading rations from ship to ship at sea. On the carrier deck, we ran, lifted weights, and told stories of our lives away from here. Hawaii seemed distant now as the ship cut through ocean swells. Life at sea was boring, especially in the North Pacific with so many older Marines aboard. There is something special, though, about a carrier making its way on the open ocean.

—

I WASN'T keen on going to Japan. Echoing the sentiments expressed in William Manchester's book *Goodbye Darkness*, the country was filled with sad memories, especially those of the battles at Iwo Jima, Guadalcanal, Tarawa, and New Britain. We sailed through the North Pacific, where the Japanese strike force had assembled before attacking Pearl Harbor. How they could have stayed hidden for so long in these rough seas undetected, I did not know.

I hadn't joined the Marines to fight in Vietnam; I now know that President Kennedy already had advisors in the country in 1962, the year I signed up, but at the time the war was not on anyone's radar. It was now—we were going to Vietnam, and everybody knew it. Except first, we could enjoy a few days of shore leave in Yokohama, taking in the sensual delights of this amazing city with all its mysteries. After leaving the purser's office, we received our shore allowance and entered the hustling and bustling Japanese city where we could forget about Vietnam and what the future might hold in store for us. I don't recall how long we were in Yokohama, but it was never long enough—a sort of a Marine Corps way of giving us R&R before the big event.

The most wonderful thing I remember about Yokohama were all the massages—in a series of rituals, the delicate Japanese masseuses would walk up and down your back. After being confined to the cramped living quarters of the ship for the better part of a month, the deep penetrating massages were a welcome change.

A week or so later, Japanese tugboats pushed the *Valley Forge* out of the dock, and we were on our way to Okinawa, the smallest of Japan's five main islands. The vibe here was very different from Yokohama, and I felt that the Okinawans didn't want us there. There were two Marine Corps bases, both historically very significant. Camp Hansen is named for Daniel M. Hansen, a Marine Corps private who received the posthumous Medal of Honor after being killed by a Japanese sniper during the fight for Hill 60 during the Battle of Okinawa. The other base was Camp Schwab, also named after a Battle of Okinawa Medal of Honor recipient, Albert E. Schwab, who died just five days short of his first year in the Marines after taking out two Japanese machine gun units.

As I told Ronna in a letter home to Hawaii, Okinawa is a special place to the Marines. Teaching us the history of the Battle of Okinawa was a good way to educate us on the tasks of the war that lay ahead in Vietnam. The stories of these two Medal of Honor recipients reminded us of the ultimate sacrifice many Marines had made, and as I wrote Ronna in 1965, "so many people died here. Was it really worth it?" Okinawa was the last major battle in the Pacific, and while I was only there for a brief period, I felt the importance of this place. One of my men, Private First Class Sweatland, got into trouble while we were there. The commanding officer wanted him punished and left in Okinawa. I talked to the company commander, and he agreed to release PFC Sweatland to me to go to Vietnam with my unit.

Ronna became my main support system while I was in Vietnam. My mother was there for me, too, but I felt that I could not share with her every day what happened on the ground because I was worried about the impact it would have on her. Ronna was different. We had just married and were in love, and I told her everything in my letters to her. Everything that happened to me must have seemed a world away to her. But the longing to be away from Vietnam was day to day, and the mail call was what kept most of us alive.

4

WHERE ARE WE GOING?

I DO NOT KNOW the exact date I boarded the USS *Princeton*, but it was some time after April 24, 1965. The *Princeton* was another landing platform for helicopters bound for Vietnam. As we approached the South China Sea, we were gripped by great anxiety. This was made worse by the soft and chilling voice of Hanoi Hannah, whose English-language broadcasts for North Vietnam aimed at US troops were aired constantly on the radio. Her haunting voice would drift across the USS *Princeton* as if she were right there on the flight deck. "Good morning, Marines," she would say. "You don't really want to go to war—you would miss your family. The American public don't want you to go either." After all these years, I still remember her talking loud and clear on the carrier as we slowly and quietly approached Chu Lai, our destination in central Vietnam. Hanoi Hannah was telling us we were going to die, which had a haunting effect on all of us.

According to the *New York Times*, Hanoi Hannah's voice was meant to chill and frighten, not to charm and seduce. We were the first to hear her broadcasts in Da Nang and Chu Lai, and I must say, it was impossible to ignore them and her message of fear. When she spoke, the carrier the length of three football fields felt still, almost too still.

I wrote to Ronna on May 2, "This is our 3rd day on this ship, and I have been feeling depressed ever since I came on board. They were not giving us any mail due to security reasons." Four days later, we landed in Vietnam. On the morning of May 7, 1965, the ship's loudspeaker commanded all Marines to assemble on the flight deck to prepare to disembark. Our commanders made it known to us that this would be the first landing off of a carrier into a combat zone by the US Marines in history. We all knew the importance of this exercise.

Each Huey had room for fifteen combat-ready Marines and an aviator who operated a .50 calibre machine gun from a wide-open door to hit back at enemy fire. I was wondering what would happen if my helicopter got hit, and I prayed as I sat on deck. As the chopper lifted off from the carrier, there was an exchange of fire between it and the Viet Cong, but it turned out to be inconsequential as the small arm firing at us from the ground was too far away.

We knew nothing about our destination when we landed in Chu Lai, but we were soon told that we were there to establish the Marine Corps' first base in Vietnam. Chu Lai was not on the map until Lieutenant General Victor Krulak chose it as a site for an airfield and named the spot with his own Chinese surname. Our purpose at Chu Lai was to secure an area to support the Navy while they were building the first runway. A month later, on June 10, I wrote Ronna, "We passed the airstrip and the area we've cleared, so the runway could be built. It gave us all a sense of accomplishment, since over a month ago, the area was controlled by the Viet Cong. This airstrip, when completed, will be almost 10,000 ft, and we will be able to land any type of aircrafts."

For the next ten months, Chu Lai and the surrounding areas would be my home, but it never really felt like home. I weighed 195 pounds when I arrived in Vietnam; by the time I left, I was down to 140. It was a beautiful place, but I felt stressed every single day. The airbase we were building was something the Viet Cong did not want. I believe to this day that they were as surprised as we were when we landed in Chu Lai.

I was an 81mm mortar section leader. A mortar section has around twenty Marines and four mortars. The mortar is a long-trajectory weapon with a three-mile range that lobs a ten-pound high-explosive round with an effective kill radius of thirty-five metres. It is a smooth-bore, muzzle-loading, high-angle-of-fire weapon used for close support of ground troops.

My section was attached to a rifle company. Sometimes I was a forward observer travelling with the front of the company, often with forward observers from artillery and support from F-4 Phantom fighter jets. I remember well one F-4 Phantom forward observer because he had been signed by the Montreal Alouettes football team straight out of university but had chosen to go to Vietnam instead. Each 81mm mortar weighed ninety-seven pounds, and oftentimes when we did not have transportation, we had to carry these into the jungle with the rifle company. The base plate alone, which the most junior members of our team had to carry while dressed in full combat gear, weighed twenty-seven pounds.

Our task was to seek out the Viet Cong and their sympathizers. By day, Vietnamese people worked the fields and rice paddies as they had for generations, but at night, many of them became Viet Cong. The Vietnamese we met each day were nice people, but we never felt accepted by them, and we never knew if they were supporters of the regime in Saigon or North Vietnamese sympathizers allied with the Viet Cong.

They say that life expectancy is short on the front lines of any war, and now that I was there, I saw why. I tried to tell that to author

Peter C. Newman, who interviewed me many years later for a book he was writing on the Canadian establishment, *Titans*. The section on me begins, "There's something strangely diffident about Terry Salman. He spent twenty-one years with Nesbitt Thomson, now runs his own investment house, Salman Partners (which has set yearly records since it opened in 1994), and sits on such national boards as Conrad Black's Southam Inc. . . . He headed St Paul's Hospital Foundation for eight years and became the most success- ful fund-raiser in the city. But at social gatherings, Salman seems distant, not quite in tune with the idle chatter billowing around him. No wonder. Few are aware of his military background in Viet- nam's killing fields, which makes standing around any cocktail party less than life-grabbing."

He went on to give a glowing overview of my time in Vietnam: "he was the first Marine in the history of the Corps to land in a com- bat zone aboard a helicopter carrier—in Chu Lai, south of Da Nang. His most dangerous assignment was the forward observer for a Marine mortar squad; those are the guys who report how close the last round came to its target, so they have to be close enough to enemy lines to take an accurate sighting. Average life expectancy for the job was one week. He earned three Purple Hearts." To cor- rect Peter, I was one of a whole brigade of Marines who landed, not the first individual, and it was one of my men who received three Purple Hearts, not me.

He then quotes me: "Vietnam was a funny kind of war. You'd go out on patrol and walk for hours or days, nothing would hap- pen, and then another patrol would go out and there'd be mines or boobytraps, all hell would break loose and a lot of people would die. One Christmas day, we had a particularly bad day as a unit, we were backed up to the South China Sea, all day I kept watching the helicopters bringing back our dead, and I remember reading that same day in the *Stars and Stripes,* the armed forces newspaper, of Jane Fonda cuddling up to Ho Chi Minh in Hanoi." Peter quotes me, "I still can't stand her."

These were not entirely my words, and when I called Peter out on it, he laughed and signed my personal copy of *Titans,* "To Terry Salman, with great admiration and respect." I had huge respect for him, too, and years later invited him to sit on the St. Paul's Hospital Foundation when I was chair.

Building one of the largest airports in Chu Lai gave us a sense of pride, but it came with a cost. The Viet Cong and the North Vietnamese army did not want us there, and every night came some sort of carnage. An attack could be as simple as a child offering us drinks, saying, "Hey Marines, want a cold Coke for a dollar?" The pop was often laced with glass, so swallowing it would lead to internal bleeding and death. We went from the bunkers to the safety of the base, but the terror of the place never went away.

My mother's faith helped me a lot during those days when there wasn't much to hope for other than leaving Vietnam in one piece. What kept me alive was the fear of what each night could bring. One night, the Viet Cong blew up six of our Skyhawk attack aircraft on the ground. The damage was done quietly and efficiently, and no one was seen or captured.

I would rotate between two weeks at the airbase in Chu Lai and two weeks on the Ho Chi Minh Trail. I was one of the few Marines that preferred the Ho Chi Minh Trail, a notorious path extending from the mountains of Laos all the way to Saigon. The trail moved people, goods, and ammunition. It was not marked; it was just there. As the Viet Cong moved from one position to another, they didn't leave any evidence except traces of blood.

The Ho Chi Minh Trail had other problems, including cobras, which bit one of our men. The only way to save him was to call in a helicopter carrier at night, whose pilot risked his life in the dark to rescue the injured Marine, lifting him back to the ship for immediate treatment.

No one really slept on the trail. As I later told Peter Newman, when I caught one of my men sleeping, I grabbed him by the throat and choked him to show him what the Viet Cong would do to him should he be captured. Whether I was at Chu Lai or on the Ho Chi Minh, there was always the uncertainty of a random attack.

I wrote to Ronna, "There is a deep hatred here built up in the Marines because of our buddies that were seen killed at the hands of Viet Cong, and I can't blame them." On June 4, the *Honolulu Star-Bulletin* put it well: "Intense heat and a blazing sun are making it rough going for the Marines as they cut supply roads, install power lines, and raise tent cities to house the squadrons who will operate from this airfield."

We spent most of the month of June 1965 building and fortifying the area around the new airfield. On June 17, I wrote home, "Myself and my men are really working hard in the hot sun because we have many bunkers to build, and it is not easy with a pick and shovel. We make the bunkers out of sandbags and trees we chopped and when we are finished, they will withstand any kind of attack. We worked from early morning to early evening." On June 13, I wrote, "If the people don't do what the Viet Cong want them to do, they will kill them. They send women and children up to the servicemen with grenades and acid-filled soda and so on. Before the Viet Cong attack, they rehearse it many times in an area similar to where they are attacking."

By the end of June, the airbase was larger, the airfield capabilities had improved—and our job securing the base had grown in size too. I wrote on June 25, "Today is Friday. It's a normal day in Vietnam, and I can't say I'm complaining very much, because I realize how rough it is and it could always get worse. Tomorrow, two or three of the companies from our battalion will take a hill that the Viet Cong are occupying. On one of these hills, the Viet Cong have holes as deep as wells, with joining tunnels so they are protected from both air and artillery attacks. Then in a few days, some South Vietnamese troops will arrive in our area to give us a hand because we have too large an area to cover and as it stands now, we are stretched out very, very thin."

Later in the same day I wrote, "Today we nearly had a very bad accident, and it was only through the will of God that no one was injured. One of our mortar sections had fired a white phosphorus round, and it landed between our position and Bravo Company. The white phosphorus will burn right through you, and it is impossible to put it out. One round weighs 10 pounds, so you can imagine how much punch it packs. They found out it was a gunner's mistake and I'm sure you'll hear about it soon. I understand a mistake such as that will take out at least four lives, so that's why we'd have to be so careful."

On July 18, "Defence Secretary McNamara came to Chu Lai twice during the day," I wrote. "All the big wheels come here, but they don't stay too long, and I can't blame them. There are better places to be." I later found out that McNamara was skeptical about the US presence in Vietnam by then and tried to push forward a peace plan privately, which is hard to believe as he was the one of the key leaders in the massive buildup of forces.

Ten days later, on the evening of July 28, our section went on patrol with our tanks. I wrote to Ronna that "I was nervous about that patrol, because it was late at night and I was afraid of landmines and boobytraps along the way. We made it back by morning OK."

As the war dragged on, it became apparent to me that our role in protecting the growing airbase in Chu Lai involved securing a vast area all the way from the South China Sea to the mountainous sections of the Ho Chi Min Trail far inland. It also became clear that

more and more villages were being infiltrated by the Viet Cong.
Whose side were the people around us on? It was very difficult to
know as they all looked the same. But as we stacked their dead bod-
ies along the side of the roads leading to the villages, it was clear
we weren't winning hearts and minds. At that point I was thinking
more about getting revenge on the Viet Cong, but the children,
women, and old people were victims, and I felt sorry for them.

We did try to earn the hearts and minds of the people, though
doing so came with risks. We gave medicine for children and
women, and food for as many villagers as we could. We worked hard
to win the support of locals. I ordered many Marines to give children food, shelter, and medical attention whenever it was needed.

On August 8, I wrote, "The Viet Cong are still very active in this
area and they are always pulling foul tricks. It's going to be their
time for a big push because surely they are losing the war and
they must do something. Last week a platoon of VC were beaten
by us in a battle. They found a dead platoon commander who was
a woman. There are also reports that one of the leading Vietnam
commanders is a woman." It also became clear that the enemy was
using women and children in battle more and more: "The women
and children are very important to the VC which is something the
West wouldn't understand. We think too much of our women and
children to send them to war." Then I added, "as long as people are
hungry, they will fight, and this is the case in Vietnam now. The
VC will fight until they take South Vietnam."

—

FIFTY YEARS after I left Vietnam, Bobby Kennedy Jr. convinced
me to go back to visit. Upon arrival at the Hanoi airport, I picked
up a small pamphlet about the battle of Dien Bien Phu, where
the Viet Minh, predecessors to the Viet Cong, had defeated the

French in a well-known victory in 1954. The pamphlet explained that men, women, and old people had carried the equipment and artillery through the mountains from Laos piece by piece to the area around Dien Bien Phu. The artillery had then been hidden in the trees to prepare for a devastating attack. I thought back to Chu Lai and the tunnels we saw there and realized that the Viet Cong had to have had the support of the people to build these incredible pieces of infrastructure. The defeat of the French at Dien Bien Phu was the end of French control in Indochina. That had been early in the war, though, and a decade later we thought we were different because we were an all-volunteer army.

On a rare day off, I took my men to a stunning beach on the South China Sea, which in another time and place would have been a resort—a plan the French had considered before the war. The sun was shining and the surf was up, so we brought out our surfboards from Hawaii and a ration of beer from the battalion's beer tent. On the way back in the afternoon, I noticed my men in the back of the trucks throwing empty wrappers and cans to the children chasing after the truck. I ordered my driver to stop, and I told my men, "Now give these children all of your food and candies, and whatever money is in your pockets." My men did not like this at all. I was trying to create good karma with the local people.

But fifty years later, when I went back to Vietnam, I was not so sure that any such gestures had much of an effect. How could a country of peasants defeat the French and then take on the most powerful country in the world? As I toured the Ho Chi Minh Mausoleum in Hanoi, I could see the answer. The North Vietnamese leader had to have had the support of all the people—even civilians—I concluded.

By July 1965, the war had started to pick up. I wrote, "I saw O'Connell today, and he is really tired and was with that company where they had 5 killed and 14 wounded." As things continued to get worse, we heard about a new enemy—the antiwar sentiment back home. On July 16, I wrote to Ronna, "I am really disappointed with how people in the world feel about the Vietnam crisis, the main one is ones in well-known colleges who hold rallies and cut down the American policies in Vietnam. They even go as far as to cut down the actions of the American troops here. I would like just once for them to spend a couple of weeks in a foxhole where the sun bakes you during the day and the VC fire at you during the night." I did not know how bad it would be until my Vietnam tour was up in January 1966. The summer of 1965 did not give us much time to think how bad the opposition to the war had become.

July and August continued to be very difficult. I wrote to Ronna, "Today, July 30, 1965, was a very sad day for us in the 2nd section 81 mortar platoon, because three of our men went into a nearby village and caused a great deal of harm and suffering and may very well have turned the Vietnamese people to hate the Marines and the American people alike. These three privates first class (PFCs) in our section went into the village and got drunk. One of my marines stabbed a woman and her baby with a knife. The woman was OK, but the 9-month-old baby was in critical condition and only by a miracle of God she would be normal, although it was doubtful. I almost cried when I heard this from Sergeant Lee. There were not too many of us walking around with our heads held high. This in turn would reflect on all the Marines over here and had torn down all the friendship we had built with the Vietnamese people. The Colonel said, 'Our platoon would work from now on; NCOs, including myself, stand guard on the offending Marine until they take him away from here.' Whatever in God's name possessed him to do this, I do not know, and I could not count the times that I told him not to go into those villages. To top it off, two Marines were killed in that town yesterday. I am fed up with all of this and will be thankful I can return to a normal life. The Marine accused of the stabbing was court-martialled in a nearby village and was sentenced to 15 years in prison at Portsmouth Naval Prison."

Although sad, this incident showed me the Marines did not tolerate attacks of any kind upon civilians, which was totally unlike what happened in My Lai, one of the most horrific acts of violence committed against unarmed civilians during the Vietnam War. On March 16, 1968, a company of American soldiers brutally killed most of the people—women, children, and old men—in a village of My Lai, slaughtering more than five hundred people. They raped and mutilated young girls and women before killing them. US Army officers covered up the carnage for a year before it was reported in the American press, sparking a firestorm of international outrage. The brutality of the My Lai massacre and the official cover-up fuelled antiwar sentiment and further divided the United States over the Vietnam War.

A few years later, in undergraduate school in Honolulu, I had an argument with my professor, who told us that what happened in My Lai was an inevitable consequence of war. I vehemently disagreed with him and told him in private what had happened to my unit on July 30. The Marines in my experience would never have tolerated anything but justice in a similar situation.

5

THE WAR
DRAGS ON

IN AUGUST, I wrote to Ronna, "The supply chopper didn't come up today because all the choppers were being used in an operation in which we had 120 casualties in the division, and we had a VC regiment trapped and jets are bombing it now." By then we had built a safe, secure space to protect the runway and the troops at Chu Lai. From an area of rice paddies, dust, and sand, we had created a base that was one of the most secured in Vietnam. And we had done it before the Viet Cong and the North Vietnamese army had gained control of the area.

That summer, almost every Marine in my unit got to go on R&R, but I always refused when asked. The thought of a few days relaxing in Bangkok, Saigon, or Hong Kong was appealing, but I did not want to leave my men. I was a corporal in the US Marine Corps, a non-commissioned officer with responsibilities far beyond my twenty-two years of age. I also did not know how I would take coming back to Vietnam. As it is, it took me fifty years to return to the country after I said I would never do so. I will carry the guilt I feel for being one of the Marines who made it back, when others did not, to my grave.

One of the opportunities I refused during my deployment was a short trip to visit Hong Kong. Another section leader, Sergeant Johnson, who loved Asia, accepted in my place. He told me Hong Kong was one of his favourite cities; he loved the night life, the teeming streets, the people, and its culture. Sadly, what happened to Sergeant Johnson on his way back haunts me to this day. On August 24, the USMC Lockheed KC-130F Hercules transport plane he was travelling in crashed into the water near Hong Kong Island, killing fifty-nine people, including Sgt Johnson. If I had gone, he would have stayed behind and lived, and seen his family again.

As I packed up his belongings to send back to his wife, I felt a sadness and guilt that I carried with me for the rest of my time in Vietnam. On August 31, I wrote to Ronna, "We are going to have a memorial service for one of our sergeants who passed away in that plane crash. We took a collection of a dollar a man so we could get his wife some flowers."

After the death of Sgt Johnson, I took over his position as section leader of the 1st Battalion, 4th Marines. I was also offered R&R, but I refused it once again. On August 30, I was told by the company commander that if I made it until my rotation in January, I would be returning to Pearl Harbor. I never saw the original orders he was referring to, but I thought I would be assigned as a military policeman. Some Marines said I was lucky because I knew where I was going and when. The unknown, of course, was whether I would survive the next five months—or even worse, if my term in Vietnam would be extended before it ended. But the August crash that killed Sgt Johnson enhanced my fear of flying even more.

—

MARINES AT Chu Lai were involved in extensive operations during Operation Starlite. By August, our pilots had chalked up

seven thousand combat sorties, with the A-4 squadrons generating between six and seven hundred flying hours per month.
Operation Starlite, from August 18 to 24, 1965, was the first major
battle of the war led by Lieutenant General Walt, a surprise attack
by the Marines against the Viet Cong and the North Vietnamese
army. The offensive was led by 2nd Battalion, 4th Marines. My
section continued to stay near the Chu Lai base, and I continued
to act as a forward observer, providing mortar coverage for our
patrolling rifle company. We were told we were advancing towards
the North Vietnamese army and the first Viet Cong regiment for
the first time in the Vietnam War. The leaders of these units had
defeated the French at Dien Bien Phu, an attack on the biggest
French airfield in Vietnam at the time, which made us aware of
how important it was to protect Chu Lai.

Later, during the first day of that operation, August 18, I wrote,
"Last night was a very sad day for our battalion because five of
our Marines were killed and 14 were wounded in a battle with the
Viet Cong... it seems like they are coming from everywhere. The
prisoners we had taken had red Chinese uniforms and their equipment was all brand new. I believe like most Marines over here, that
for every injured Marine we'll make the VC pay." As the war esca-
lated in the fall of 1965, I continued to lose weight from the fear of
the unknown and the extensive activities that our units engaged
in. Guerilla warfare is very stressful; you never know when or from
where the next attack is coming.

Meanwhile, the airbase at Chu Lai was acting at full capacity
and every day I prayed that I would survive my last ninety days in
Vietnam. That three-month period turned out to be five months.
At that point, I was 140 pounds, but I lucked out on September
5: "I was surprised that Sergeant Lee had smuggled in all kinds of
civilian food from the staff mess sergeant," I wrote to Ronna. "You
see, this food is supposed to be for the big wheels. Anyways, we

had real eggs, bacon, and franks with two large loaves of bread. I ate so much I hardly ate breakfast the next morning. It seems like a long time since I have had real food."

Sergeant Lee was the first Black friend I had ever had in my life. But he was going to leave Vietnam soon. I first met him in Camp Pendleton, where he had been an MP patrolling Highway 5, the fifty-mile stretch of road between Pendleton and San Diego. He was a career Marine and an NCO. He had a wife and son that I hoped to meet someday but never did. He was just happy to leave Vietnam, which he did in mid-December.

—

THERE WERE other casualties of war, like Marines who had not heard from their partners back home, only to find out that they were having an affair with someone else. And then there were the "Dear John" letters, where spouses or girlfriends decided that they were going to move on. In one case, I recommended to the company commander that a man be allowed to go home for humanitarian reasons.

At Ronna's funeral in July 2021, I thanked her for her support during those terrible months in the summer and fall of 1965.

—

IN MY office in Vancouver today is a picture of me and sixteen other Marines who were with me during those last few terrible months. I think of each of them from time to time. The Marines have always been able to blend people together from all walks of life and then mould them into the finest fighting force in the world.

There was Allan, who had servants in his parents' mansion in Nashville and graduated from Vanderbilt University. He was soft-spoken, well educated, respectful, and followed orders.

Then there was Private Smith, who loved the Marine Corps but loved to drink more. He was also violent with women when he was not sober.

Then there was Jones, who took the picture, who joined from Chicago, because, according to him, the judge gave him two options: join the Marines or go to jail. I can still remember him clearly, killing rats in our bunker with his Ka-Bar knife. The bunker was filled with rats from the food the Army of the Republic of Vietnam left behind. Many of us preferred to live outside the bunker and expose ourselves to enemy gunfire, but not Jones.

Then there was my radio operator, Boyd, who served two terms in Vietnam. He was a fastball pitcher with the Baltimore Orioles farm team who taught me how to play baseball. After catching his fastballs for thirty minutes, my hands were blood red and sore. He was a classic old-school pitcher, overweight around the middle with a cigarette always dangling out of his mouth, and a cool guy to have on patrol as he would navigate the jungle looking for the Viet Cong and its supporters while we called in mortar fire.

Then there was Private Butcher, who barely met the Marine Corps height criteria. He was strong as an ox and able to carry that twenty-seven-pound mortar baseplate for miles. He was the guy who fell asleep on the Ho Chi Min Trail, prompting me to choke him to warn him what the Viet Cong would do to him if they found him snoozing there.

Private Fowler was a quiet Marine, who always did what he was told.

Private Looney came from the South and was still fighting the Civil War, and he didn't get along with Private May, the only Black man in my section.

There was Private Ladd, who was from Kentucky and always made people laugh. He loved the Marine Corps and rarely had anything negative to say about anybody.

Private Grant was a real "squared-away" Marine, muscular and good-looking in his uniform.

And Bill, who always wore his hat on an angle and kept mostly to himself. He didn't talk much and just did his job.

Then there was another private whose name escapes me, who wore a Marine Corps tattoo on his right arm. Some Marines called him Four Eyes because he wore glasses. He carried his rifle with him everywhere.

I have often wondered what happened to the sixteen people in that picture who were my men. As the antiwar sentiment continued to grow after our return, most of us subconsciously decided to bury what we had fought so hard to gain. Sadly, for me this meant forgetting about my fellow Marines, the men who fought with me. All I know for sure is that when I visited the Memorial Wall in Washington thirty-eight years later, I did not see any of their names carved into the stone, which made me happy.

—

AS MARINES know, when you become a short-timer, you start counting the days left on tour. But the departure day is always an illusion, so ticking off days on a calendar, as most of us did, caused more stress than it eased. I kept writing home to Ronna that I would be leaving in December of 1965, but I wasn't always optimistic.

It wasn't just the fighting. The psychological effect of being at war affected everybody. I had one man practise Russian roulette with a .45, which as every Marine knows is impossible as, unlike a .38, this pistol doesn't have a revolving chamber. So he pointed a loaded .45 at his temple and shot himself in the head before falling into my radio operator's chest. I wasn't able to share this story with anyone, then or ever until now. It was too painful to talk about, so I buried it for a long time. I liked to believe that it had never happened. The sadness I felt when this Marine took his life was really hard to process.

Nothing about Vietnam was predictable. The months through the fall of 1965 found me longing to go back home to Honolulu to be with my new wife. I ached for that little apartment on Ke'eaumoku Street, where I could study and listen to Dean Martin on 78 rpm records.

I wrote home, "Life at times becomes very depressing and meaningless. At this moment, out in the ocean, I can see them bringing in more troops from the carrier *Iwo Jima*." Even though I loved the Marine Corps, I only survived because of the deep faith that my mother had raised me with, and the support of all my men, including officers like Lieutenant Valley and Lieutenant Myatt.

On the night of October 27, 1965, we were attacked by the Viet Cong and the North Vietnamese army, who tried to penetrate the airbase at Chu Lai. It was a night I will never forget. The enemy destroyed four Skyhawks and severely damaged another six aircraft. We killed fifteen enemy soldiers that night, in an attack I had feared for a long time.

On November 14, I wrote, "My dearest Ronna, today is Sunday. I just came back from church. You should see the new chapel we built. Inside the aisle way is red brick and so is the altar, and the seats are put in the white sand outside. It has a slanting roof and stands in the middle of a grove of trees. They plan to build a bronze memorial for all the men of 1st battalion, 4th Marines, men who lost their lives in Vietnam. It would be placed outside the chapel."

That fall I again saw Lt Valley, who had been with me since Kaneohe Bay, when he had recommended I be promoted to corporal. He gave me the highest recommendation any officer could give, and he really wanted me to become an officer after the war. But at the time, that would have required me to give up my Canadian citizenship. In Vietnam on December 1, 1965, I was appointed a sergeant of the United States Marine Corps. When the battalion commander presented me with my stripes, he said, "I want to congratulate you especially because it is very seldom that a man with as little time as you have at the Corps makes sergeant."

Marines are promoted by what is called a cutting score. This is the number of points you have earned in your time in the Corps, based on your rank, your conduct at your job, your accuracy with your rifle, your physical fitness, and the additional training courses you have undertaken. Some Marines believe that the number of pull-ups you can do enhances your score. As Josh Freedman wrote in *Chron*, "Rising through the ranks of the Marine Corps to make Sergeant is a lofty goal, one that few enlisted Marines will achieve; it could take years of competence, professional behavior, and careful preparation."

On December 4, I saw Lt Myatt, our new company commander. He asked me if, now that I was a sergeant, I was going to stay in the Marine Corps. I told him it was too hard to be just married and away from my spouse. I had been with Lt Myatt since Kaneohe Bay in Hawaii, and he had landed with me at Chu Lai on May 7. He was a born leader who would go on to make a career in the Marine Corps. I would say goodbye to him in January 1966. Two months later, he was awarded a Silver Star in Operation Oregon. During that battle, my old unit suffered nine deaths and forty-one wounded. Lt Myatt successfully maneuvered his platoon and coordinated an attack against the Viet Cong. He went on to become Major General Myatt and the commander of Camp Pendleton in California.

Perhaps MG Myatt's greatest role, however, was honouring Gold Star parents and families at the Marine memorial in San Francisco, which he did for thirteen years. At the 2018 gala, he vowed that he would "never forget the men who died under his command." He broke down before continuing his speech. He had come a long way from the time in a barber shop in Chu Lai when he saw a Marine getting a small trim and asked the soldier if he was a short-timer in Vietnam. The Marine replied "No," so Lt Myatt told him to "Sit down and get another haircut."

December 1965 was a grim time for me as I anxiously waited for my rotation out of Vietnam, which was now only a month away. On December 18, I wrote, "We were moved to an area down by the sea. I am really happy I'm rotating as this is not a very nice place." As Christmas approached, I witnessed one of the grimmest sights of my life: "It is saddening to watch the choppers bring back our dead and wounded from the big battle not far from here." In the eerie stillness, the only sound I heard that day was the choppers. One by one, I witnessed helicopters landing and Marines taking out our dead and putting them in body bags to carry to our trucks to drive slowly to the makeshift morgues in tents nearby. I was grateful our pilots had risked their lives to bring back our dead. But that sight will haunt me forever.

I thought to myself, the families of the fallen probably don't know what has happened and won't know until around Christmas, as the Marine Corps has to process and identify the dead and wounded. I prayed and cried and later that day wrote, "This Vietnam is not a very pleasant place and it hurts even more to pick up a newspaper and see people supporting the Viet Cong by carrying a Viet Cong flag at various places. It causes you to wonder who you are really fighting for." "Victory to the Viet Cong," said one poster along with the Viet Cong flag. And Joan Baez sang "Where Have All the Flowers Gone."

The only positive things to happen that December were receiving thousands of Christmas cards from Americans and going to a Christmas show with Bob Hope, Anita Bryant, Joey Hetherton, and others. The actor Hugh O'Brian also came to see us one on one. These small acts of kindness gave us a glimmer of hope.

I spent New Year's Day, 1966, in Chu Lai and left a few days later for Da Nang, a large port city on the South China Sea that was a major air hub during the war. As I flew out of Chu Lai, I remember looking back at the huge complex and feeling proud that we had created a massive air base from a landscape of rice paddies and scattered villages. Today, Chu Lai is the third busiest airport in Vietnam and the largest in area, at thirty square kilometres.

As I left Vietnam, I thought of all my fellow Marines who would never make it home alive. When a Marine dies in combat, two officers in dress uniform make a painful visit to the parents or spouse of the deceased. They walk up the driveway leading to the house where those who have lost a loved one wait, knowing what they are coming to say.

I have never seen this in person but can only imagine what it would feel like to those who have lost a loved one on active duty. It causes me to tear up as I know the scene is only the beginning, and it would play out over and over again after I left Vietnam. At times I wished it had been me and not them. But the pain would not stop with the parents or the spouse—it extended to the children, the grandparents, the cousins, and uncles, and so many more. I knew that when I talked to the spouses who had been left behind. And I knew it when I visited the Memorial Wall in Washington, DC, decades later and saw extended families searching on the granite slabs there for the names of their relatives who had died.

This is why when I go to a hockey game in my hometown of Vancouver and they play the American national anthem, I put my hand over my heart. I know I am a Canadian, but at that moment I remember my brothers who I have lost, and I am American too.

6

FINALLY
LEAVING VIETNAM

THE TEN-HOUR FLIGHT from Okinawa to Honolulu seemed to go on forever. My fear of flying had developed at Chu Lai and slowly got worse as the airfield grew from one small runway to over ten thousand feet. It came at a great cost to me. I was flying on Continental Airlines, an iconic American brand; the aircraft had an orange stripe from the middle to the tail with a black sign saying "Continental" on top. The flight attendants were gracious and helpful during the long flight, where I was anxious about what lay ahead. I felt so fortunate to be flying back to Honolulu to see my wife, Ronna, to whom I had only been married a few months before going to Vietnam, but every time the aircraft ran into turbulence, I shook.

But no amount of turbulence could have predicted what happened to me on my arrival at US customs in the Honolulu airport. After seeing I was a sergeant in a Marine Corps uniform, the customs officer proceeded to turn my duffle bag upside down and ransack every item. He was looking for something, most likely drugs. But it was his manner that was most offensive. It was almost as if the antiwar sentiment was on display at the customs checkpoint. He made me empty my pockets, and he patted down my uniform. With an ironic twist, he did allow me to keep my Ka-Bar and pilot survival knife. In a strange way, I was grateful to him because my Ka-Bar was my prize possession, particularly if my rifle ever failed.

A Marine was awarded the Navy Cross recently for his heroics in killing several of the enemy with his Ka-Bar in Vietnam fifty years ago. "Lance Corporal Stogner's machine gun team leader was severely wounded. Four enemy soldiers dragged the wounded Marine... into a nearby treeline where they began to torture him. Lance Corporal Stogner, despite his own painful wounds and with complete disregard for his own safety, pursued the enemy into the treeline to rescue his fellow Marine. After his service rifle malfunctioned, he used his Ka-Bar fighting knife to kill the enemy soldiers, then picked up his machine gunner and the machine gun, and carried them back to friendly lines." While I never used my Ka-Bar in hand-to-hand combat, I was happy to have it back when I thought the customs agent was going to confiscate it.

After customs finally let me through, I entered Honolulu airport to find Ronna waiting for me. She had borrowed her stepfather's station wagon and asked me if I wanted to drive. I said yes. In the sixties, there was no H-1 freeway from the airport to Waikiki, so I drove along the Nimitz Highway, named after Admiral Nimitz, US Pacific Fleet Commander in Chief during World War II. As I made my way towards the Aloha Tower, I had to pull off the highway because I was shaking so much. I told Ronna that it would be best if she drove. I was six-foot-one and 140 pounds, and I had started to break down. The Vietnam War was finally over for me, but the pain and the guilt would linger for a long time.

7

STATIONED
IN PARADISE

THE ANTIWAR SENTIMENT was everywhere but less pronounced in Hawaii, which I was happy about. After three weeks' leave, I reported to Marine Barracks, US Naval Brig, Pearl Harbor (in the age of political correctness, it was later changed to US Naval Correction Pearl Harbor). The Pearl Harbor base is rich in history and one of the most prestigious duty stations in the Marine Corps. As I drove up to the gate, I thanked General Walt, who had sent me there, as my fellow Marines in Vietnam had told me my new job was a dream posting and almost impossible to get.

As a Marine Corps MP waved me in at the entrance to the base, I felt very lucky. The white-and-red buildings looked whitewashed and clean in the Hawaiian sun and yet had a feeling of having been there a long time. The parade deck was immaculate, and the trimmed grass surrounding the area looked pristine. It wasn't a place to hang around; it was a place for pomp and ceremony on special days. Pearl Harbor is sacred ground for Americans and the site of the national memorial and resting place for the 1,177 sailors and Marines killed on the USS *Arizona* during the attack on Pearl Harbor on December 7, 1941.

I had been appointed assistant warden at the US Naval Brig, a medium-security prison for Navy, Marine, and Coast Guard prisoners who had committed minor infractions. The duty was twenty-four hours on and forty-eight hours off, so for a young married man living in Waikiki, it was a dream. I had a cot in my office, and if we didn't have to book any prisoners, which was most of the time, I could get a decent night's sleep. The steel gate to the prison was just outside my office and must have been an imposing sight for those who had to be confined.

One prisoner I felt sympathy for was a corporal in the Marine Corps who worked at Camp H.M. Smith. He was a bartender at the base who had apparently had an affair with an officer's wife he met when she was having a drink at the bar he worked at. Having an affair with an officer's wife is a violation of the code of military justice. He was demoted to private and given thirty days in the brig. The charges written in front of me suggested that she had approached him, but I guessed that it had been consensual.

Another prisoner's crime was taking his girlfriend out to a restaurant and trying to charge the bill to a room that he had not booked. One long-term prisoner was a suicide risk who had to be watched all the time. He had been caught sneaking a razor blade into the cell by hiding it between his buttocks.

But that was as exciting as it got. And in 1965, after Vietnam, I really enjoyed this duty. On my days off I could spend time at the beach with Ronna, play handball at the courts at Fort DeRussy off Saratoga Road in Waikiki, and enjoy the extensive nightlife after the sun went down. We had our own black patrol wagon and driver that we used to pick up prisoners in Waikiki. We worked with the Honolulu Police Department—the HPD made famous three years later by the television program *Hawaii Five-O*. The Vietnam War was in full swing, and there were many servicemen and -women stationed in Honolulu as part of the troop buildup, so life was always interesting.

Patrolling the Waikiki streets with my driver was a bit of a high for a twenty-three-year-old—and a long way away from Vietnam. Our black Ford truck had roll bars with flashing lights to help exercise our authority. As we turned down Kuhio Avenue and then down the Ala Wai Canal, life felt pretty good. I'd quickly gained back the weight I'd lost in Vietnam and was back to my 190 pounds.

With the military equivalent of a search warrant, we knocked on an apartment door on the Ala Wai Canal only to be greeted by a naked woman who said, after we presented her with the search warrant, "He is not here sergeant, but you can look if you want." After looking in the apartment we left.

The first apartment Ronna and I lived in together was on Kuhio Avenue, near the Kuhio Theater and next to the Waikiki Jungle, a dense five- or six-block area of modest or rundown apartments that was quiet in the day but turned into a party place in the evening. This tiny enclave was the centre of the city's counterculture. The residents were suspicious of government and wanted to live a care-free life free from authority. It was not a place my driver and I patrolled alone at night, and neither did my friends at HPD. It was a tough neighbourhood where AWOL sailors and Marines would often hide. Our deal with the HPD was that they would control the civilians and we would try to control the servicemen. In the blurry evenings of heavy drinking and partying, there were a lot of fights, and handcuffs became more of a necessity as the night wore on.

The rest of Waikiki was like an urban paradise, dense with palm trees and lush vegetation. It was easy to get distracted by the views and the smells of the tropics. Our apartment was right in the middle of the nightlife scene, so my days off made life in

Hawaii magical. We often listened to live music at the Banyan Tree in front of the Sheraton Moana, where Arthur Godfrey had a radio program, *Hawaii Calls*, that ran from 1935 to 1975.

Marine Barracks Pearl Harbor was a plum duty station given to a few lucky Marines returning from Vietnam, often as an enticement to convince them to sign up for four more years. Most Marines didn't get sent to Hawaii twice, but I was one of the lucky ones. My initial four-year term had been extended by four months due to the war, and I was now in one of the most prestigious duties available. I was grateful.

In the movie *From Here to Eternity*, there is a scene in which a ship is pulling out of Honolulu Harbor and Karen Holmes (played by Deborah Kerr) says, "If you throw a lei out to sea and it does not go to shore, you will never return to Hawaii; if it goes to shore, you will return to Hawaii someday." My lei had definitely hit the shore. And my life in Hawaii was about to get better as we moved into our new apartment and I entered Chaminade College, now the Chaminade University of Honolulu. This was made possible by the generous support of the GI Bill and my in-laws.

In October 1966, I left the regular Marine Corps, though I remained a reserve until I received my honourable discharge on June 18, 1968, six years after I had signed up. It was a sad day when I received that formal document, which still hangs proudly in my office near the picture of the letter signed by General Walt giving me orders to leave Vietnam. My experiences in Vietnam and the way the American people had turned on us veterans had soured me on making a career in the Marines, but I never lost the pride of being a Marine, which in my heart I will always be; no one can take that away from me. I turned in or gave away all my uniforms, including my dress blues, the hardest to part with. I closed a chapter of my life I never wanted to end. I was a Vietnam veteran, and nobody cared.

Terry's aunt and grandfather with Terry's great-great-grandmother, circa 1939.

ABOVE LEFT: Baby Terry in his mother's arms, studio portrait, 1942.

ABOVE RIGHT: Tal Salman (Terry's father), studio portrait, 1939.

TOP: Terry and Ronna in Hawaii, Christmas 1964, just before Terry was shipped off to Vietnam.

BOTTOM: Terry on military leave, in Montreal with his dog, Laddie, 1964.

TOP: Lance Corporal Salman, studio photograph, 1964.

BOTTOM: 1st Battalion, 4th Marines, Chu Lai, Vietnam, August 1965. Terry is seated on ground, front row, left.

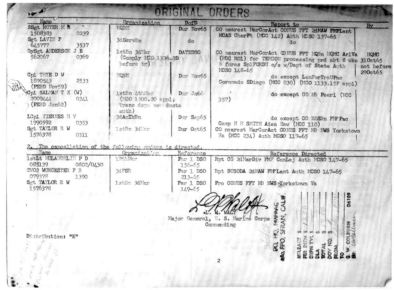

TOP: The Ho Chi Minh Trail, located in the mountains appearing at the top of photo. The view is from Hill 69, a fortified US military installation, which overlooked the activities of the Viet Cong, circa 1965.

BOTTOM: Terry's orders to leave Vietnam, signed by Major General Walt, 1966.

Brian Aune and his son Jonathan (Terry's godchild), circa 1985.

Terry with Brian Aune and Brian Aune's wife, Ruth Glenen, at Terry's retirement party, February 2011.

Terry telemark skiing, Whistler, BC, 1987.

Terry with his two daughters, Tasha and Krista, at the Chilkoot Trail, 1991.

To Our Favourite
CHAIRMAN OF THE BOARD
- FROM -
ST. PAUL'S HOSPITAL FOUNDATION STAFF
DECEMBER 1994

TOP: Terry on motorcycle, surrounded by St. Paul's Hospital Foundation staff, December 1994.

BOTTOM: With Lauren Bacall, Orpheum Theatre, Vancouver, February 1995.

Terry with his wife, Chris Salman, on his sixtieth birthday, 2002.

Sitting with his grandchildren, left to right: Amber, Esme, Naiya, Terry, and Hugh, 2021.

It wasn't until much later, when I was in my sixties, I was standing outside the Hyatt Hotel in Indian Wells, California, with a hat on that said "Marines 1775" that a young man came up to me and thanked me for my service. I said, "You saw the hat," to which he replied, "We all did—thank you for your service, sir." I thanked him and almost broke down. I had waited forty years to hear that.

I enrolled in Chaminade College in 1966 as I didn't want to leave the Hawaiian Islands just yet. After Vietnam, I didn't want to expose myself to the antiwar sentiment and race riots on the mainland. Chaminade was a small liberal arts college founded by Father Chaminade, a Roman Catholic priest who survived persecution during the French Revolution and founded the Society of Mary, whose members were priests called Marianists.

The Marianists are both a lay and religious order, incorporating the work of the religious order and parishioners, devoted particularly to education. At Chaminade, there was a painting of the wine barrel that Father Chaminade hid in to avoid being captured during the French Revolution. Father Chaminade was unique in creating what was known as a sodality where Christians and lay people gather together, male and female, young and old, under the patronage and protection of the Virgin Mary. Although I am Anglican, the teachings of Marianists had a profound impact on me.

After the Vietnam War, I was trying to figure out how religion fit into my life. Although I still had my faith, I had some doubts, but going to St. Andrew's Cathedral in Honolulu helped a lot because the faith-based activities enabled me to spend time with believers who shared my values. I met people from all walks of life, and we spent time studying some of the theological issues I was learning at Chaminade. Often, I would go to Punchbowl, the National Memorial Cemetery of the Pacific, to look at the graves of those who had died in Vietnam, including people I had known. Punchbowl is in a beautiful setting, and while it is a cemetery, it is peaceful.

I was a business major, and my courses and studies were largely in liberal arts, literature, and philosophy. These studies had a profound impact on my life. The Roman Catholic brothers at Chaminade taught me how to reason; philosophy was at the core of their teachings. To name a few, we studied Thomas Aquinas, Kierkegaard, Bertrand Russell, Kant, and Michael Scriven. My faith, which my mother had instilled in me, was severely tested by the death and suffering I had witnessed during the Vietnam War. Chaminade was like an oasis, with the white walls of Spanish architecture, open windows, and enclaves where you could sit between classes and enjoy the tropical breeze. For a vet like me, it was a wonderful place and time for healing.

The Roman Catholic brothers at Chaminade taught me how to think, but they never pushed their religion on me. Rarely did I leave class without thinking more about whatever we had discussed. Does God exist, and how can we prove it? They taught me how it was possible to prove that God does not exist, as Michael Scriven argues in his powerful book *Primary Philosophy*. But the brothers taught me that, as with Thomas Aquinas and Kierkegaard, at some point, as a Christian, you have to make a leap of faith. In a presumption of arguments, the brothers noted in discussions of alternative theories, there is no argument that points to a slight chance of the existence of God, so the only alternative is atheism. Still, the brothers made a strong case for faith-based belief. During one of these discussions, one of the older brothers pointed out to the class that miniskirts were distracting.

—

ON MARCH 7, 1969, Ronna gave birth to our first daughter, Tasha, in Queen's Hospital in Honolulu. She was a beautiful, healthy baby, born in such a happy time and place, and Ronna and I could not

have been prouder. To pay my way through university and support a wife and baby, I accepted a position as a dormitory advisor
at the Kamehameha Schools, one of the most prestigious private
schools in the world; to go there, you have to be at least part native
Hawaiian. The school was funded entirely by the Bishop Estates,
who own about 9 percent of all the land of the Hawaiian Islands.
Most of this land is not for sale but leased, like much of the land in
Waikiki—once the lease expires, they re-lease it for a much higher
price. The estate's endowment is larger than Harvard's and Yale's
combined. To Hawaiian families, admission to this school is coveted, and acceptance is selective.

Ronna and I lived in Unit 21-C of the boys dormitory with six-
month-old Tasha. In our kitchen, we once left our baby Tasha
unattended, only to have her tumble from the counter to the
concrete floor below, a few feet from a small fridge stacked with
Heineken beer purchased from the military PX at a steep discount
(I still have privileges there). We were in a state of shock as we sat
together on the couch not believing what had happened. We didn't
take her to the doctor, having heard somewhere that babies are pli-
able. We kept Tasha awake for a few hours and kept checking if she
was okay. From that day on we never went anywhere without our
daughter, even taking her to restaurants where she would sleep
on the seat between us in a baby carrier. We treated the concrete
floor of the apartment with a new respect and caution for the rest
of the time we lived there.

My sole purpose, as a dormitory advisor, was to make sure the
boys were supervised while they were in the dormitory. I liked this
position a lot, because as a Marine Corps veteran, I felt at home
working with boys. They were only a few years younger than
Marine recruits.

Kamehameha Schools was a fun place. The boys at my dorm
filled me with happy moments. They were so generous to me. I

once asked one of them whether it would be possible to see the Don Ho show at the International Marketplace. Getting admission was an impossible task for most people, especially on the weekends, but Ho—a very popular Hawaiian singer—was a Kamehameha graduate, and in no time at all, there we were, sitting in the front row, being greeted by Ho himself.

If you had the brains to go to Stanford medical school, Kam Schools provided the funding and the scholarship, and if you wanted to be an aircraft mechanic, they had the engines to train you.

Hawaiians are very proud of their culture, and anyone who has studied or worked at the school has a very special status. Years after I left the islands, I returned to Hawaii on honeymoon with my second wife, Chris. After spending the afternoon at Sunset Beach on the North Shore of Oahu, we returned to our rental car only to find it was stuck in the sand; the five-litre Ford Mustang had all the weight in the front and little in the back. After trying to push it out myself without success, I noticed three Hawaiian boys drinking beer in a truck and asked them if they could help me. I was greeted with silence, not once but three times. As it was getting dark, I reached out to them for help again: "You know, boys, I used to work as a dormitory advisor at the Kamehameha Schools." Suddenly they stepped out of their truck, said, "Hi, brother," and proceeded to help me push the car out with smiles. Had they not helped me, we probably would still be stuck there.

On that same trip, Chris and I visited the Honolulu Museum of Art and admired the numbered prints by Hawaiian artist Herb Kawainui Kāne, many of which are on display in the Outrigger Hotel in Waikiki. The sales lady told us they were sold out, but when I told her that I had been an advisor at the Kamehameha dormitory, she said, "Give me a moment." She returned shortly after with Kāne's fiftieth out of fifty artist proof prints, hand signed. If you have a history with the Hawaiian people, it is good for life.

With the antiwar sentiment everywhere on the mainland, the sprawling six-hundred-acre Kamehameha School grounds was a good place to hide from my Marine Corps past. While there I learned about the rich culture of the Hawaiian people and how important it was to preserve it. The teenage boys accepted me for who I was, and I don't think I ever told them that I was a veteran. I ate with them in the somewhat formal dining room and enjoyed my fellowship with them. If we wanted to play football, I would turn on the lights on the football field, and we would play for hours. While they tried to pull tricks on me, being a Marine Corps sergeant had taught me a few tricks of my own.

—

IN 1969, I graduated from Chaminade, having received several accolades as a student, including acceptance into Delta Mu Delta, an international honour society founded by professors at Yale and Harvard, and inclusion in the *Who's Who* publication of universities and colleges in the United States. My academic and overall performance gave me the prerequisites to apply to any graduate school. I thought about applying to Harvard Business School or Dartmouth College's MBA program, but I did not have the financial resources at the time. But I applied to many others and was accepted at several, including the University of Hartford Graduate School of Business (now the Barney School of Business) and the New York University Graduate School of Business Administration (now NYU Stern School of Business).

I was tempted by NYU because the famous professor Peter Drucker, who wrote many iconic books including *The Effective Executive* and *Concept of the Corporation*, taught there. But in the end, I decided to attend Hartford because we had a small child and the school housing in downtown New York was very limited. The

University of Hartford was in rural Connecticut, and we moved into a place close to Miss Porter's School, a private prep school founded in 1843, and enrolled Tasha in a preschool taught by the students at the school. The university also offered me a teaching assistant position, which gave me some additional income.

Before we moved to Connecticut for the second time—after bouncing back to Hawaii via Vancouver for a spell—Ronna and I spent several months again in Vancouver in a small rented apartment on Comox Street in the city's West End. We had three hundred dollars in our bank account and our two daughters were toddlers. We thought of living in Vancouver as Ronna was born there, but I had no job and the city was expensive. But we loved to walk along the beach at English Bay. I have wonderful memories of this area, but I made the tough choice to send my two daughters and Ronna to Montreal to live with my parents. My first stay in Vancouver was short and ended abruptly.

Connecticut was a magical place to live in those days. The university itself was founded by Mark Twain's wife, Olivia Clemens, and Elizabeth Colt, wife of Samuel Colt, the creator of Colt firearms. It had an attractive campus, and we were lucky to live close by. Katharine Hepburn's house was just a few minutes away. Connecticut was rich in culture with a flourishing arts community, making it a nice place to live with a young family. Ronna and I welcomed our second daughter, Krista, who was born in Saint Francis Hospital in Hartford on April 15, 1970.

The university had outstanding professors—many of whom were tired of living in busy cities and wanted the pastoral lifestyle this part of Connecticut offered. Because the university also had a night school, many executives who lived in the area enrolled in the program to complete their MBA. Many of them had taken their undergraduate studies at nearby Ivy League schools.

Hartford was rocked by a number of protests and riots in the late sixties. I avoided the antiwar protests—I wanted to bury all my memories of Vietnam, never think about it again. But I felt a lot of sympathy for the anti-racism protestors after the horrible prejudice I had witnessed in the American South, and I attended several demonstrations to show solidarity with them. Hartford was also a place of extreme racial intolerance. I remember going to East Hartford for a protest that turned into a race riot and feeling totally comfortable among the Black people and their grievances. I listened to the fiery speeches and saw people throwing petrol bombs in anger. The contrast between the idyllic campus we lived close to and the depraved North End, the centre of all the riots just twenty minutes away, was striking.

While I finished my studies, I worked part-time as an analyst with a money manager in Avon, Connecticut, one of the wealthiest parts of New England, where worth was often defined by the size of your house and property and the history of your family. George, the fund manager, got me involved in all aspects of his business, leading up to making the final investment decision. I met many Wall Street types, who came up to Hartford to solicit our services, and I got to taste, for the first time in my life, the fine food the expense accounts allowed us to enjoy. I was wined and dined like I was somebody, and even enjoyed my first trips to legendary Wall Street. I had been to New York briefly as a student to visit NYU, but now I got to see the heart of North American finance up close for the first time.

As I was getting close to graduating in 1973, the yearning to return to Canada, which I had left a decade earlier, grew stronger. My parents were getting older, and I had not seen them or my brothers or sister for a long time. So I started asking around for people with contacts in the banking world up north.

I was introduced to Tony Beck, the owner of *The Bank Credit Analyst,* a monetary publication based in Montreal that we subscribed to. He gave me some references to banks in Montreal, where I had the potential to work. I was studying, working two jobs, and helping Ronna bring up two children, so the only time I could go for an interview was Saturday; I didn't want to skip school to go up to Montreal or Toronto. I wrote to all of Tony's contacts, and the only one that would see me on a Saturday was Brian Aune, the heir apparent of Nesbitt Thomson. Little did I know how our meeting would change my life.

8

A MENTOR
SECOND TO NONE

I T IS HARD to underestimate Brian Aune's role in my life. He gave me a chance when other opportunities were not forthcoming. He did something rare—he took a personal interest in seeing that I was given an opportunity to enter the investment business in Canada after living in the United States for over twelve years. He took me into his life as family and provided me with a support network. To top it all off, he later made me godfather to his only son, Jonathan, which he claimed, "spoke volumes of what he thought of me."

Brian was one of the most respected investment bankers in Montreal. I first met him in the winter of 1972. I was set to graduate the following summer and was considering giving up my green card and moving back to Canada. Thanks to Tony Beck's introduction, Brian Aune suggested we meet one Saturday at Bar Maritime in the Ritz-Carlton in Montreal, a block from McGill University on Sherbrooke Street. I knew the Ritz-Carlton as a legendary hotel, and the Maritime as a bar where politicians and prominent businessmen met regularly. It was a place to be seen and meet people. I hadn't lived in Montreal for twelve long years and was looking forward to living in a big city again. I was also looking forward to wearing a suit and tie again.

I got up before dawn on the Saturday and drove my 1955 Nash Rambler north on I-91 from Hartford to Montreal in a blinding snowstorm. It was snowing so hard it turned into a whiteout, so I had to keep stopping and getting out of the car to make sure the windshield wipers were working because I could barely see in front of me. The Rambler was two-wheel drive with snow tires, so it was slow going, and the more I drove the fewer cars I saw. What was normally a five-hour drive took seven, but I was just grateful I didn't end up in the ditch.

Although I had seen pictures of Brian, I couldn't help but wonder what he looked like. Most of my discussions had been with Ruth Glenen, his executive assistant, who later became his wife. Even on a Saturday, Brian wore his traditional dark-blue suit. He looked like a cross between Clark Gable and Errol Flynn, with a charm that was second to none. Deane Nesbitt had nominated Brian as his successor at Nesbitt Thomson, the powerful stock brokerage firm founded in 1912. But you would never know it by looking at Brian's business card, which discreetly said "assistant to the president." Brian Aune and Thomas Kierans now run the company, though I never met Tommy in those days. It would be one of many meetings I would have with Brian in the Maritime bar.

For some reason, Brian took an immediate liking to me. He arranged numerous meetings for me with money managers and other investment firms over the next three months, but after spending more and more time with Brian, I really wanted to work for *him*. In the end he hired me because he could sense that and wanted to move on as he was very busy. I was supposed to be hired temporarily but never sensed that would be the case; I ended up staying for the next twenty years.

Before graduating, I was up in Montreal every second weekend. Brian introduced me to the legendary nightlife of the city, taking me to many well-known restaurants and bars. We never waited in line because he was so famous in the finance world; most business executives knew him as a leader at a time when Montreal was the financial capital of Canada and Nesbitt Thomson had its head office there. The bouncers who controlled the doors to the most popular discotheques and bars would call him to the front of the line and say, "Good evening, Mr. Aune, please come in."

In the early summer of 1973, he said something to me that would stay with me for the rest of my life: "If I can't hire a Canadian who was a US Marine Vietnam veteran, what good am I?"

Thanks to my two jobs, I managed to graduate from the University of Hartford without any debts, an achievement I was very proud of. I also received some good references. The most notable one was from Professor John S. Lazar, who wrote:

> I have known Mr. Salman . . . as a person of outstanding intelligence, strong professional motivation and excellent financing judgment. His poise, personal stability and tact convince me that he is uniquely qualified for a professional future that calls for a combination of analytical insights and an ability to deal with people. He is a fine communicator who projects well his powerful achievements.

In Ian Fleming's book *Thrilling Cities*, the only Canadian city he mentions is Montreal, alongside Hong Kong, New York, Tokyo, Rome, and several other major metropolises. When I first visited it after twelve years in the US and Vietnam, I rekindled my love for the city I had left as a young man. I loved its stunning architecture and old-world charm draped with history, in particular Old

Montreal, the site of the first Canadian bank at 32 Rue Saint-Paul, and James McGill's house on Notre-Dame Street. Simon Fraser the fur trader lived in Old Montreal for a while before he embarked on his epic journey across the country, which culminated in his descent of the Fraser River to its mouth at what is now Vancouver.

In the summer of 1973, we moved to Montreal and rented a townhouse in Dollard-des-Ormeaux, not too far from the two-and-twenty highway, which became my commute to downtown. The Nash Rambler died that summer when I pulled into a gas station near my new home only for the brakes to fail when I pumped them. Tasha was four years old and Krista was three.

From 1973 to 1979, Brian and I had dinner together at least twice a week. One of his favourite restaurants was Carmen Chez George, which had a sign upstairs at the entrance that read, "Adults at play." On any given night, you could see René Lévesque there with his wife Corinne, Peter Mahovlich of the Montreal Canadiens, and Peter Thomson, the son of the founder of Nesbitt Thomson. It was impossible to get a seat in this place unless you knew somebody—but everybody knew Brian, so our evenings were regularly interrupted while he said "Hi" to an endless parade of people.

Before I contacted Brian, I had been watching the political crisis in Quebec. During the October Crisis in 1970, the FLQ kidnapped British Commissioner James Cross, and within the next two weeks they had killed Quebec's Deputy Premier Pierre Laporte. Robert Bourassa, the premier of Quebec, asked the federal government to intervene. Prime Minister Pierre Trudeau enacted the War Measures Act and sent in the army to deal with the unrest. The military occupation was controversial, but Trudeau prevailed. In the famous dialogue with the news reporters who questioned the validity of engaging the army, he said, "Just watch me."

Two events that month affected my interest in the mining business even though I was only just entering graduate school in

Connecticut. During the October Crisis, a protester in Montreal threw a rock through my father's McGill office on University Avenue and destroyed the elaborate blown-glass device he had used for his PhD thesis. The thesis and his equipment were related to the chemistry of metallurgy; he had used them to examine flotation, how mineral molecules attach to the surface of air bubbles. This is an important process used in the mining industry to extract valuable ore from waste rock.

The second event occurred in the same month, a few blocks away from the head office of Nesbitt Thomson in Old Montreal, on the corner of Rue Saint-Jacques and Rue Saint-Pierre. A second protester threw a rock at a hundred-year-old Tiffany-style stained glass mural that depicted all of Nesbitt Thomson's business across the country, including the mining business that the company had financed. My dad's lab equipment was never rebuilt, and Nesbitt Thomson's stunning mural was covered by a black curtain, never to be opened again, although it was not damaged. The French separatist protesters singled out English institutions and neither McGill University nor Nesbitt Thomson, to my knowledge, took a stand against them.

The October Crisis was the beginning of the end of Montreal's reign as the financial capital of Canada. In the years that followed, several of our departments moved to Toronto. The shining brass plate of Nesbitt Thomson's name remained, but the office in Old Montreal became a fallback to a bygone era, as did the Old Montreal stock exchange building, which now houses the Centaur Theatre.

Back then, St. James Street, where my first office would ultimately be, now called Rue Saint-Jacques, was the street that financed Canada, home to the head offices of RBC, BMO, the Molson Bank, Royal Securities, and a number of trust companies that are still there today. The head office of Nesbitt Thomson was at 350 Rue Saint-Jacques. My office was on the third floor. The Montreal fire marshal told me I had to keep my desk at an angle so people could walk past it to the fire escape below. The fire escape always looked a bit shaky to me, and fortunately we never had to go down it. Through the window at night, we could see the beautiful large cross that stands on Mount Royal and is lit up at night. There are many versions of how the cross got there. The one I like the most is: one of the founders of the city, Paul de Chomedey de Maisonneuve, asked God to spare the city from a disastrous flood and promised that if He did, he would personally carry a wooden cross on his back to the top of Mount Royal and erect it there. Today the cross is a large illuminated steel structure that can be seen from miles away.

Three years after the October Crisis, as I sat in Nesbitt Thomson's boardroom, I looked at the life-size murals painted by Canadian Pacific artists as they travelled across Canada. The paintings were interesting for several reasons. First, they were not painted on canvas but on the wall itself. Second, I could not help but notice the paintings of Cominco's mine in Trail, BC, which was acquired by CP Rail from a previous company called Consolidated Mining and Smelting, a rail client of theirs who could not pay its freight bills; such was the boom and bust of the mining business, in so many ways. Yet today, the Cominco mine is more important than ever as many of the metals it produces make the world greener, like copper, silver, and gold. Looking at these beautiful paintings in the boardroom, I had no way of knowing that my first mining client was going to be Cominco.

The Montreal nightlife was the best in Canada, and after a trip to Toronto, we could not wait to catch the flight back to Montreal to enjoy the rest of the night, which would last four hours after Toronto had closed its bars. The centre of the action was the ten-block radius from Sherbrooke Street to Sainte-Catherine Street, and University Avenue to Crescent Street.

Brian ran Nesbitt Thomson, and I was a research analyst, covering a number of companies such as Canadian Pacific, Canadian chartered banks, and the cable companies. I liked research a lot and was allowed to make investment decisions as I saw fit. Brian often did interviews for key positions in the company, and I would tag along. Everybody liked Brian, who made you feel at ease, and he was a skilled financial banker trained by Clarkson Gordon & Co in Vancouver. Deane Nesbitt, the company chairman who was planning on retiring soon, was a Presbyterian and rarely socialized after work. Accordingly, Brian did most of the interviews and socializing in the evening, notably with executives from Trans-Canada Pipelines and Power Corporation, accounts that Brian supported. After we finished work around 7 or 8 p.m., we would go out to dinner, and it was then we met many of the key people who would ultimately run Nesbitt Thomson. The people who thought the evening was finished after dinner were in for a surprise.

One of my favourite interviews was with Joe Oliver, who worked at Merrill Lynch. Brian invited him out because he was considering hiring him to head the investment banking department of Nesbitt Thomson. After dinner, Brian turned to Joe, who thought the evening was over, and said, "So, tell me Joe, how would you run the corporate finance department?" A fair question, though it was nearly two o'clock in the morning. I wasn't at the dinner, but Brian told me afterwards that Joe gave such a good answer that he hired him right away, which he rarely did. Joe later became minister of finance under the Harper government.

9

A PATH LESS
TRAVELLED

RESEARCH WAS THE guts of our institutional business, a department where it was sink or swim. My evolution as a research analyst was pure luck. I owe my good fortune to Brian Steck, who was then the director of research. He said, "Go to the library upstairs and find something you can research that is not covered by any other analyst." By sheer luck, I discovered that no one had covered Canadian Pacific, because of the complexity of the company and its many subsidiaries, which were involved in a whole variety of business areas.

This discovery was a defining moment in my career. I became a transportation analyst covering CP, spending many months in 1974 researching and editing a hundred-page report on the company, one of the largest individual company research reports that Nesbitt Thomson had ever compiled. Up to that time, the only research report I had produced was on *Ripley's Believe It or Not!*

After visiting the company in Toronto, I accidentally left my draft research report in the taxi on the way to the airport. Brian Steck was not impressed, but fortunately we had kept a copy, and I redeemed myself with a new draft. Then Lawrence Bloomberg, head of the institutional equity department, tore that one apart line by line. The research department at Nesbitt Thomson was a tough place to work—the standards were very high.

Despite his criticism, Lawrence decided that my report had potential and helped me put it back together. We burned the midnight oil on St. James Street to produce a readable format and an investment recommendation that said, "CP was the story where the parts were worth more than the whole." The report was finally published and would go on to be known as a bible in my circle. But first, Lawrence and I were off to Chicago, where a number of large investors were located.

Lawrence took a plane to Chicago, but even eight years after returning from Vietnam I was still paralyzed by the thought of flying and opted to go by train instead. The train I took was called the Super Continental and ran between Montreal and Chicago, from 1955 to 1977. It was an elegant train with a first-class dining car and comfortable sleeping compartments that enabled you to have a good sleep as the train rolled along the tracks. The bar had comfortable swivel chairs covered in leather. As I sat down in the dining car, a woman asked me if she could join me. The evening was very pleasant as the snow continued to come down. I loved the sound of trains as I fell asleep, but to my horror I woke up soon afterwards to find the train was headed back towards Montreal due to a snowstorm. Until a plow came and cleared the tracks, our train was sidelined.

I finally arrived hours late in Chicago with my boxes of CP reports. Lawrence Bloomberg was not happy. After reaming me out, he and I pounded the streets of Chicago, visiting numerous institutions, occasionally telling them about the train trip. That was the last time I took a train on any Nesbitt Thomson business trip. After Vietnam, I did not fly commercial until 1974, when Terry Jackson, one of our institutional salespeople, flew with me to Boston. I still remember approaching Boston on that flight; it was very turbulent, and I was nervous and sweating. My fear of flying ran deep, but I had to face it; my days of train travel for work were over.

After my marketing research trip to Chicago, I was chosen by the Government of Canada to act for the Royal Commission on Corporate Concentration, created by Prime Minister Pierre Trudeau on May 1, 1975, to research CP. To celebrate, Deane Nesbitt and Brian Aune invited me to lunch at the Mount Royal Club, a prestigious private business club founded in 1899, where the waiters wore tuxedo jackets and white gloves. I had never been to a restaurant this fancy and felt a bit out of place as a young analyst still wearing suits from Tip Top Tailors. The Royal Commission staff explained the process and what they were looking for. The report was published later that year with a glossy cover showing a number of CP businesses on the front. Sadly, I no longer have a copy.

I first met Ian Sinclair, chairman and CEO of CP, in 1974. He was an imposing figure, sometimes known as Big Julie. We became friends after the *Montreal Gazette* called me and asked what I thought of his salary of $350,000 a year. Under the Railway Act, Ian was not required to disclose his pay, but the Securities Exchange Commission (SEC) of the US had other ideas and eventually forced him to disclose it. The next day, the *Gazette* quoted me in bold letters saying, "Ian Sinclair, a bargain at $350,000 a year." His assistant later told me she had put the paper on his desk for him to see.

My research on CP revealed that the company Ian Sinclair had built was one of Canada's largest blue-chip investments that we believed was only trading at a small portion of its value. This value was recognized by Paul Desmarais, the CEO of Power Corporation. Upon listening to my presentation on CP, Paul decided that he wanted to own it. After some negotiation, Ian Sinclair allowed

Power Corp to buy up to 20 percent of the company. After our meeting, Paul, Brian, and I had dinner to celebrate. After dessert, Paul said to us, "You'll have to give me cash for the taxi, because I don't have any money." He of course was referring to cash on hand at that moment.

10

MENTORS BY
THE HANDFUL

NESBITT THOMSON'S RESEARCH department in the seventies was a powerhouse. I was a new hire they did not need. Every office was taken in a firm that oozed tradition. I was there because Brian Aune had brought me on. One morning as I entered the building, I saw one of the brokers pulling up outside our office in a chauffeur-driven Bentley. I wanted to be here, and I wanted to be like him.

When I was first introduced to Hubert Marleau, he said, "Why should I interview you? You've already been hired." The next thing I knew, he was pushing a roll of toilet paper down the research department floor that read, "Vote for Hubert Marleau for Director of Research," and laughing with a high-pitched voice. Hubert was one of the five research analysts in that department who later left to create their own brokerage firms; his firm was called Marleau Lemire. Hubert was an economist, and a good one at that. People listened to him, and he was entertaining. There was a serious side to him, but I rarely saw it. That's what made him a good economist. The world of investment research is very tough, and Hubert excelled in it.

At Nesbitt Thomson, Hubert also covered the Canadian chartered banks, an area he handed off to me and Bob Dorrance, who we hired straight out of McGill, so Hubert could focus on being an economist. Afterwards, Hubert said I was a better bank analyst than he was, but we were both good storytellers. The last time I saw Hubert was on the Seawall in Vancouver's Stanley Park in the nineties, when I heard the same high-pitched voice saying, "Is that the incredible Terry Salman?"

Our most notable publication was a series of individual, cellophane-wrapped brokerage reports on each Canadian bank focusing on their LDC (less-developed countries) loans exposure. After the report was published, it received wide distribution in the *Wall Street Journal* and many other papers. Then Deane Nesbitt, our chair, received a call from the VP of finance at RBC, who said, "You should fire the two idiots who produced that research report," Bob and me. Deane replied, "I'll get back to you."

Deane called us down to his office and asked us where we had found our information. We told him that we had got most of it from the Montreal public library and by talking to the lead underwriters, most of whom were on Wall Street. He then called RBC back and said that if they could provide the information to prove us wrong, we would publish a retraction. No such information was forthcoming, so our careers were saved, and the reports stood as published.

Deane Nesbitt was an iconic figure, a war hero who was wounded flying a Spitfire in the Battle of Britain during World War II. He was awarded the Distinguished Flying Cross and knighted by the king for his bravery. He came back to Montreal after the war to run the brokerage firm his father had started. The president of McGill University student society, he became a noted financier who went on to finance the TransCanada Pipeline. His wife was a descendant of Senator William McMaster, the founder of

McMaster University. To be around Deane Nesbitt was like being around royalty. His insistence that Bob and I not be punished for the report, as the Royal Bank wanted us to be, enabled us to continue our careers and build our own brokerage firms. Bob sold his firm, Newcrest, to TD bank for $225 million in 2000. As for Deane, he never did retire from Nesbitt Thomson; a few years after I joined the firm, he died in a skiing accident on a hill he owned in the Laurentian Mountains north of Montreal.

Lawrence Bloomberg, the head of our institutional equity department, went on to become one of the most successful brokerage firm entrepreneurs in Canadian history. In 1979, he created First Marathon, an innovative discount brokerage firm that he sold to National Bank two decades later for $712 million, around $1.1 billion in today's dollars, while becoming the largest individual shareholder in National Bank. People said that Lawrence suffered from short-man syndrome, but he was a force to be reckoned with when he marketed our research. From his elevated trading desk at First Marathon's head office in Toronto, he could be seen barking out instructions to his traders. He was an incredibly smart man and fun to work with.

Patrick Mars, who had just left our research department when I joined, had created Bunting Securities, which ultimately became Bunting Warburg, a global player in the financial world. Monty Gordon, who joined the institutional sales department before me, went on to create Gordon Capital, the first firm to create a bought deal that enabled other firms to compete with global players. It was a startling innovation that is still extensively used by underwriters today.

Tom Kierans, who ran the research department at Nesbitt Thomson before I joined, became a prominent financier in his own right, first with Pitfield, MacKay, Ross Limited, where he joined with Lawrence Bloomberg, then with ScotiaMcLeod.

Covering the Canadian banks entitled you to attend a luncheon with the senior bank officers once every quarter, which included a gourmet meal accompanied by the finest Canadian wine. It was our time to ask the bank officers any questions we had about their operations. It was a big improvement from C-rations in Vietnam eight years earlier. It had other benefits too.

I started to learn about the mining business through CP's ownership in Cominco and Fording Coal, two companies I acted for later when I became an investment banker after my move to British Columbia. Many years before, in high school, I had worked a couple of summers at Gaspé Copper Mines, a subsidiary of Noranda mines in Murdochville, QC, as a labourer in the mill laying tailing pipe—a back-breaking job.

Research was easier work, and I liked it a lot, but it had its risks and challenges. Getting too close to management sometimes clouded your vision. You always had to take a step back before making any recommendation. Covering large companies has less risk, but in the end you are looking to make calls and make investors happy. A good investment report takes at least one to two months to complete, and at Nesbitt Thomson, we took pride in our reputation as being among the country's best researchers. In certain sectors, such as the mining business, we were better than that—we were among the best in the world.

But by 1979, I had reached as high as I could go in research. I was ranked number one in transportation, covering CP and its other public companies (known as CP Investments), and was somewhere among the top five in the banks. I felt like it was time to try something new. So I went to Brian Aune in the latter part of 1979. He suggested that I move to Vancouver, get an apartment in Calgary, and cover the oil and gas sector for the firm. I liked the plan, so Ronna and I decided to move west.

—

THE CANADIAN Pacific train known as the Canadian was the last stainless-steel passenger car purchased by the company from the Philadelphia Budd Company. I had always wanted to travel on that train, and Ronna did as well, as she wanted to see a friend in Sault Ste. Marie. So we decided to go west in style, and we rode with our daughters from Montreal to Vancouver. The elegant train meandered its way through Northern Ontario to Winnipeg, where it met up with the Toronto portion of the train.

The elevated observation car, named after Canada's national parks, gave us a Canadiana trip second to none. As the train travelled through Saskatchewan, you got the sense of the breadth of the country, with wheat fields and grain elevators as far as the eye can see. The sleeping compartments were cozy, and our two young girls bunked up behind the red velvet curtains. The train worked its way up through Alberta to Banff, where we got a look at the breathtaking Rocky Mountains. Even the children enjoyed it. Ronna and I got off for a short stop at Lake Louise, and as we were taking a walk, we noticed the train was moving with our daughters still sleeping onboard. Fortunately, it was only minor engineer work being done on the train.

The highlight of the trip was the spiral tunnels near Kicking Horse Pass, a miraculous engineering feat built to navigate the train through the incredibly steep terrain of the Rockies. As we entered the dining car on the last day of the journey, heading into BC, I could sense the history of this train and its importance to Canada.

—

FOR THE next six years I spent four days a week in Calgary and three days in Vancouver. In Calgary, I got an office across the street from the Westin Hotel (then called the Calgary Inn), which is now the Alberta regional office of TD Bank. I loved that office on the corner of 4th Avenue and 3rd Street. It was in the hub of the city, and the Calgary Inn was a legendary spot where so many key businesspeople stayed when they came to town. I flew home on the weekends to visit Tasha and Krista, then returned to Calgary on Monday or Tuesday, depending on the workload. I would meet my assistant, Martine, at Umberto's restaurant in Vancouver and map out my work plan for the week before catching the plane to Calgary.

Calgary was a lonely place for me. Ronna and I separated not long after our move to BC, eventually to get divorced; she and my children remained in Vancouver. We were kids when we got married, but we were fortunate enough to have two wonderful daughters, and while she and I grew apart, we always remained friends.

With no social life to distract me, I was working twelve-hour days and using every major law firm in Calgary on investment banking transactions. It was a good time to be in the oil patch. Brian Aune had told me, "If you do nothing else, get us the Dome Petroleum account." I did, and it soon became our biggest account; it would eventually pay us about $8 million in fees in the 1980s, around $30 million today. I was doing deal after deal with companies like Turbo Resources, Aquitaine (a subsidiary of Elf Aquitaine, a French conglomerate), and CDC, to name just a few. My lawyer, John Burns, used to keep a tombstone of every transaction I completed on the wall of his office. In all my years in the investment banking business, this was the period of my life when I generated the most transactions, at a time when Nesbitt Thomson was competing against major global players (this was before banks were allowed to own investment dealers).

We were generating so much business that our competitors were all over us like vultures, saying we did not have enough capital. We had to produce abbreviated financial statements to show that we were indeed solvent or a going concern. The investment banking business can be brutal sometimes.

The first time I met Bill Richards, the president of Dome, I could not believe how gracious he was. Here I was, an investment banker with little experience except as a research analyst, who had taken a demotion to come to Calgary, of all places. My biggest transaction to that point had been helping Dome acquire a 53 percent stake of Hudson's Bay Oil and Gas. Bill told every banker around Bay Street to put up billions of dollars on a handshake. In those days, no banker could get enough of Dome Petroleum. When I put up our fee proposal to him, Bill put his cowboy boots on his desk and said to one of his colleagues, "Terry must be angry with us." He then traded us off our proposal against Goldman Sachs, who were sitting in the next room.

But Bill liked me, and I never sensed we would lose the deal. He just wanted us to be competitive. The company's CFO, Peter Breyfogle, told my partner Brian Aune, "Terry pushes us just enough, but not to a point of discomfort." This was just one deal with Dome, and many equity offerings followed, including a couple of private placements with subsidiaries like Musketeer Energy, which Bill had created and loved. It was the time of the National Energy Program, and Dome was the biggest player. I was so busy marketing with Dome Petroleum that I missed my brother's wedding, but I did not forget my mining clients in Vancouver.

One afternoon in Calgary, while I was working on a couple of transactions involving trust companies, I stopped in at a trendy

Italian restaurant on 4th Avenue to grab a meal. Sitting a few tables away from me were two attractive women. One of them, Anne O'Farrell, said to her friend, "If that man looks over here one more time, I'm going to ask him to join us." I was looking for some company, so I accepted their invitation to sit with them for dinner. Later in the evening, when Anne went to the lady's room, I asked her friend out.

My date was Jill Koshure, who worked as an executive assistant to a VP of Petro-Canada. She helped me weather the lonely times in Calgary and cope with the loss of my parents, both of whom had died by the early eighties. Jill was a welcome surprise in my life and made the long winters in Calgary bearable. Most importantly, all of my clients loved her. It was nice to have someone to talk to, and she was such a fun person to be around at the Calgary Stampede.

Nesbitt Thomson had rented an apartment for me—the Franklin House, a few blocks away from the Ranchmen's Club and only a fifteen-minute walk from my office. It was in a nice area from a bygone era filled with large old trees and wide sidewalks. One day as I was walking to the office down Centre Street, I noticed a Ferrari dealership. I went in and asked the salesman the price of the 308 convertible, the car made famous by Tom Selleck in the TV show *Magnum, P.I.* I liked it so much I gave him a thousand-dollar deposit and told him I would be back after my workday to finalize the payment.

The Ferrari 308 stayed at my apartment in Calgary for a number of years. One time as I was entering Banff National Park, the young woman at the ticket booth was so eager to ask all about the car that she created an angry line of people waiting behind me. A year later when I was driving back to Vancouver via Jasper Park Lodge, the attendant told me I could park my car downstairs. I told him I couldn't leave it unattended, so he gave me a bungalow and told me to park it on the grass in front.

—

IN 1980, before I started to get involved in community service, I was like most young investment bankers—self-absorbed and focused on accumulating things, and after working so hard, enjoying life by travelling, skiing, hiking, and attending the ballet. I decided I wanted to hike the West Coast Trail (WCT), in Pacific Rim National Park on the west coast of Vancouver Island, after reading that it was a hike like no other. Back then the trail was more primitive than it is now, as I discovered when I did it a second time a few years ago.

The WCT stretches along the coast from Port Renfrew to Banfield. I took a young investment banker, Doug Pocock, one of the three exceptional young people who worked for me in Calgary. "I'll do it with you," he had said eagerly, not knowing much about hiking—or tides, which are crucial aspects of this particular seaside hike. We both ventured out to the Graveyard of the Pacific, an area known as such for its treacherous coastline. Doug is almost seven feet tall, and I could see right away that his height was a hindrance in navigating the deep surge channels, especially when the tides were coming in. I remember telling him to jump from one large boulder to another to avoid falling into the ocean. A day earlier, an Indigenous guide at Port Renfrew had taken us out in a small boat to the trailhead, but getting to the trail was also tide-dependent. Even though I had spent sixteen months at sea in the Marine Corps, I knew nothing about tides, and Doug knew even less.

We were told by another hiker, who was coming from Banfield, that it was more interesting to take the ocean trail than to go through the woods; the views were spectacular, and there were better places to camp overnight. As we made our way from the trailhead towards the beach, we navigated steep ladder systems like we'd never seen before. The next morning, we hiked for eight hours along the boulders of the coast, trying to keep aware of the tides with our tide table. As the tide came in hours later, we were to look for a rope that was hanging from a tree, that would lift us up from the surge channels to higher ground. On the beach that night we camped, and we continued in this way along the trail for the next five days.

One of the most picturesque beaches we stayed at was Tsusiat Falls, where a waterfall met the surging Pacific Ocean. It was spectacular and one of the few places where we could take a shower. It left such an impression on me that I flew over the same site years later in my plane and took a picture of the waterfall below. From the air it is even more spectacular because you can see the fresh-water river heading towards the falls. Later, we worked our way through the Nitinat Narrows, where Parks Canada had chartered Indigenous fishermen to take us across the waterway, and for a few dollars we could have some fresh halibut when we reached the other side.

I never thought of myself as being better than anyone in those days, but I certainly felt I had surpassed my former self, as I had grown by leaps and bounds. I was taking on more responsibilities at the office, with more and more people working for me in Calgary and Vancouver, and I was focusing on the education of my two daughters and the quality time we spent together hiking, skiing, and travelling. I still remember climbing over the rocks to find the safety rope; when I asked Doug if he could see it, he said he was looking still. The WCT enabled me to look back on my life and look forward to the future, which seemed so bright at the time as I waited for my assistant to pick us up at Banfield. As Ernest Hemingway, one of my favourite writers, once wrote, "There is nothing noble in being superior to your fellow man, true nobility lies in being superior to your former self."

11

LIFE
LESSONS

I MADE LOTS OF friends in Calgary, like Dallas Hawkins III, who ran a company called Oakwood Petroleum. Dallas was a veteran like me, a US Navy frogman who had fought in World War II. On February 17, 1945, prior to the landing of the Marines in Iwo Jima, he was one of a hundred members of the underwater naval demolition team dropped from small landing craft within seventy yards of the island controlled by the Japanese army. Dallas and his colleagues surveyed and dismantled landmines. They travelled lightly, only carrying Ka-Bars, mine detectors, and demolition equipment. They were often fired upon by the Japanese soldiers on the nearby beaches. For his efforts, Dallas was awarded the Bronze Star, the third-highest medal the US Navy offers. He always wore a miniature ribbon of that star on his left suit jacket lapel. It was that kind of risk-taking that gave Dallas the strength and courage to try new ventures. It is no wonder that Jill called him a "larger-than-life" character. Oakwood Petroleum acquired thirty million barrels of sweet Alberta crude oil that was very financeable. Goldman Sachs did the debt, and we did the equity.

Dallas and I were friends and spent a lot of time together. Like me, he commuted to Calgary for work, in his case from Spokane, Washington. One time we went on a trip to the Gaspé's Cascapédia River in Quebec, fly-fishing for salmon in a private lodge. Famous American families have fished this river for generations. It was very different from fishing on the West Coast; you cast from a small boat and might wait hours before landing any salmon. It was not long before Dallas caught his first salmon. On the way back to Spokane in a private plane, we dropped off Dallas, only to find when he cleared security and customs that his fish was gone. After some reflection, he said, "Well, they probably needed it more than I did."

Dallas always had a sense of humour, and he was always a very optimistic person. He made me laugh all the time and was a master of one-liners. One time, he told me that he would give each one of his three children a million dollars before he died, to see how well they managed their money. He taught me to appreciate the small things in life. Dallas loved to travel as I did; at that point in my life, I was the second-most-travelled person on Canadian Pacific Air Lines. At that time, I acted for CP Air on the acquisition of 40 percent of Fording Coal's interest, which was owned by Cominco.

I went forth and back between Calgary and Vancouver most weeks from 1979 to 1985. In Vancouver, most of my clients were in mining, the largest account being Teck Resources, which ultimately bought Cominco from CP after Ian Sinclair retired. The new CEO of CP was William Stinson, who I always called Bill. He, Donald Carty, and I had the idea to take CP Air public, with the hotels included in the new company. It was a brilliant idea because it meant the airline's volatile earnings would be offset by the more stable hotel earnings. The airline business was tough, and Bill Stinson did not have the same attachment to it that Ian Sinclair had.

I called Bill and asked him to meet for dinner to discuss the idea. He told me that he was going to a CP board meeting—"Let me take a look at their prospectus and then we can have dinner." Of course, whenever you met with the CEO of CP, you had to have dinner at one of their hotels. We ate at the Hotel Vancouver, and I showed Bill the prospectus we had ready to file. He told me that he was going to sell the airline after the board meeting because the numbers looked so awful.

—

I FIRST met my second wife, Chris, in 1982 on a flight from Vancouver to Toronto. I was sitting in first class, and she was working the shift. That was the golden age of air travel, and although she had a university degree, she had chosen to become a flight attendant. It was hard to beat five-day layovers in Rome, Lisbon, and other exotic destinations. I was sitting next to Bob Kadlec, then the president of BC Gas (now FortisBC). We were en route to a fishing trip on the Cascapédia.

When I asked Chris what she did in her spare time, she said she spent most of it with her boyfriend. A few months later, however, on another flight from Vancouver through Calgary to Amsterdam, I asked a flight attendant who had her back to me if I could have a newspaper. When she turned around, I saw it was Chris's friend Angie, who commented that I had yet to have my meal. A few minutes later, Chris came back with my breakfast. She told me she was going to be in Vancouver soon, and did not have a boyfriend anymore, so she would be available to have dinner with me. We were engaged not long afterwards.

Across the street from the coffee shop where we were sitting was Birks, and that's where we purchased Chris's engagement and wedding rings. I was fond of Birks as it was a very well-known company to Nesbitt Thomson. I remembered so well the Birks store at Phillips Square in Montreal that makes all their jewellery in a shop downstairs, so I just had to buy it from them. That branch of Birks at the corner of Georgia and Granville streets is now London Drugs, though the Vancouver Block clock tower is still there.

Chris was an accomplished athlete, having set several national records in swimming. My favourite trophy of hers is a silver cup she won in a one-mile swim in Stony Lake, Ontario. She beat everyone, including the boys whose parents had invited her family over for the weekend. As Chris tells it, they were never invited back.

On May 6, 1983, we were married in Toronto. On our honeymoon in Kauai in Hawaii, Chris wanted to take a flight around the island. I told her she was on her own; I would wait for her until she came back. I hadn't been in a helicopter since the last time I'd flown in a Huey in Vietnam, in January 1966. It would take me another ten years to overcome my fear and get back in a chopper.

—

TWO YEARS later, we took the first of many trips to Italy. Chris knew Italy well, having spent many layovers there when she was a flight crew member for Canadian Pacific. We made a stop in Milan, where I purchased the only truly custom road bike I have ever owned: a Cinelli Supercorsa. It was a work of art. In that shop, they made everything custom, especially the frame, which was measured to my specifications, including weight, height, and arm and leg length. The frame-builder was Mario Camilotto, a legendary figure in the business in the eighties. The serial number is 8540: for being the fortieth frame built in 1985. They also sized up in detail the handlebars, which were wrapped in leather, with drilled out brake levers. The bicycle was a work of art. It is no wonder that Umberto Menghi, the well-known Italian restauranteur in Vancouver, told me I could bring the bike into his restaurant any time during lunch. He was not the only notable person who recognized its value. Malcolm Parry, the *Vancouver Sun* writer, also rhapsodized about it when he was writing about me riding it up Cypress Mountain.

—

I FIRST met Joe Oliver when Brian Aune hired him as the head of corporate finance for Nesbitt Thomson in Toronto. Joe was a McGill-educated lawyer and Harvard MBA with an incredible wit. In the tough world of investment banking, Joe was a great guy to work with who made the long nights and excessive travel all worth it. He had the best vocabulary of anyone I knew, even if I did not understand some of the words he used. Joe went on to work for First Marathon as the head of corporate finance with Lawrence Bloomberg, then went on to be the president of the IDA, where we worked together again when I was on the board and, later, the chair.

Joe has an amazing sense of humour. There was never a time I met Joe and he did not make me laugh. My favourite Joe Oliver story is when Chris and I played golf at Angus Glen in Markham, Ontario, with him and my partner Tom English. The course was going to be used for the Canadian Open a week later, so the grass off the fairways had been left very long to challenge the pros. Sensing this would be a difficult day on the course, I suggested that I share a cart with Tom, who had a low handicap, and Joe could sit with Chris, who I hoped would be a calming force on him. Each time his ball ended up in the tall grass he would try to hit it out, only to find it wouldn't go anywhere. Joe said, "That's not fair!" and threw down his club in frustration... and we were only on the first hole!

Years later when he was finance minister in Stephen Harper's government, a government aide asked Joe why he was jaywalking.

He replied that it was a way of life as a Montrealer. Joe was the last finance minister in Canada to balance the budget. He was fortunate to have followed Jim Flaherty, the only Canadian finance minister in history to have a state funeral. They both believed in strong fiscal management. When I left Nesbitt Thomson years later, I missed Joe but we kept in touch. Joe and his wife, Golda, married in Philadelphia, which was significant to me because the Marine Corps was founded at Tun Tavern in that city in 1775. I visited the historic plaque where the tavern used to be when I was there for his wedding. I also went to one of his sons' wedding, and he came to one of my daughters'. We loved to ski together in Whistler; before his knee gave out, he came every year. I generally let him ski with my wife, Chris, and he would argue with her and my daughter Krista that he knew his way out of the mogul field. These days Joe writes thought-provoking articles for a number of publications that are too easy to dismiss. Unlike most pundits talking about politics, he is not really a spokesperson for the Conservative party—in fact, I don't think they even listen to him.

In Calgary, I had Bruce Ramsay working for me. In October 1985, Bruce and I acted for CP in the acquisition of Nordair. Bruce was one of the only people we were able to hire in my history at Nesbitt Thomson from Wharton School of the University of Pennsylvania, where he received his MBA. We got lucky; when the head investment banker at Wood Gundy was supposed to interview Bruce in Toronto, he gave the task to a junior banker, which caused Bruce to say, "I'm going to work for Terry." The first time I called him at the University of Pennsylvania, I heard a garbled message: "This is Bruce Ramsay, leave a message." It sounded like he had been drinking. Bruce was an incredibly smart banker, but very eccentric. He came out to meet me in Vancouver and agreed to join my team, but not before having two lunches at Bridges in Granville Island; he had not eaten in days and was making up for lost meals.

My favourite picture of Bruce was when he was on the front page of the *Calgary Herald* windsurfing in the middle of winter. I convinced him to move out to Calgary, which he was familiar with as he came from Nelson, BC. Unfortunately, he was not able to bring the girl he loved from the US. She wanted to get married, and Bruce never believed in marriage; to my knowledge he never got married, though he did have four children.

Bruce worked with me on numerous transactions. During his first winter working for me, I told him he could no longer wear his North Face shell to business meetings, and I gave him an old trench coat of mine, which he wore every day for all the years we worked together. Years later he emailed me to invite me to his fiftieth birthday party. I wasn't sure I could make it, but he was not going to take no for an answer, telling me he would send a plane to take us up to Banff. In addition to the obvious, he said, "I am inviting everyone who has ever had a role in my life." Bruce went on to create Acumen Capital, which he ultimately sold.

12

MINING WAS
IN MY BLOOD

IN 1985, BRIAN Aune asked me to hand over the responsibility for Calgary to Mac Van Wielingen because we were acquiring Deacon Hodgson and he needed me in Vancouver full-time. From then on, I mostly covered the mining sector, developing a large base of exploration companies active in the Western United States and the Pacific Rim, including Australia, Indonesia, and Japan. At this time, we created the first mining team at Nesbitt Thomson. We hired Egizio Bianchini and several seasoned veterans to augment our corporate finance and research presence. On March 4, 1994, we launched the first mining conference at Whistler, BC, which is now the most prestigious mining conference operated by BMO in Florida. The attendees at the initial conference included some of the largest gold companies in the world, including Barrick, Newmont, and Kinross.

My interest in mining started with my father working in mining towns. I often travelled with him, sometimes in a car, occasionally on a horse, to visit his mining clients and students. I still think, today, of mining headframes as an artform. Years later at Salman Partners, I gave an oil painting of a wooden headframe to Norm

Keevil as a gift for allowing me to do the first bought deal preferred share of Teck Resources in the 1980s. That deal was the
largest preferred share offering for a mining company up to that
point. I have a picture of Chris Simpson and me giving Norm
Keevil a $50 million cheque. Later, when I decided to terminate
Salman Partners' Investment Industry Regulatory Organization
of Canada membership, and essentially stopped being a broker
dealer, Norm Keevil brought that painting to the dinner that Ross
Beaty, Brad Cooke, and other mining executives hosted for me.

I never told Norm, but not too long after that transaction, Chris
Simpson, who was the youngest investment banker we ever hired,
took his own life after checking in to the Pan Pacific with his Nesbitt
Thomson BMO discount. This was long before mental health was on
anyone's radar. Years later, his wife told me that he once told her he
did not know if he could continue doing this. Investment banking
was a tough job in those days, and juniors like Chris worked hours
and hours, sometimes up to sixteen hours a day, plus weekends.

—

MY PRACTICE in mining started with Canadian Pacific interests
in mining companies. Nesbitt Thomson did not like exploration
companies at the time, because of the risk involved, but Teck
was large enough for them. The larger mining companies paid
the bills as I tried to convince Nesbitt Thomson to finance junior
exploration companies. One day after returning from a business
trip, I attended a closing dinner, an investment banking ritual
to celebrate the closing of a financing. When I got to my table
at Umberto's, I found that I was seated next to the director of a
company called Orvana, one of the first underwritings of a junior
under Nesbitt Thomson. He introduced himself as John Patterson,

and when I told him my name, he asked if I was any relation to Professor Salman. It turned out that he had been my father's first PhD student at McGill University, and he was now the head of metallurgy at Queen's University. John went on to work for Robert Friedland, who convinced him to leave Queen's after many years.

Before the evening ended, I invited John to attend my daughter Krista's graduation at McGill, fifty years after my father graduated with his master's in mining engineering. Much to my surprise, John drove from Kingston, Ontario, to Montreal to celebrate Krista's achievement. Sadly, he passed away from a heart attack while he was working with Robert Friedland. I still appreciate his attendance at the closing dinner at the Ritz-Carlton hotel that evening, that outdoor setting with the legendary swans swimming in front of us.

Norm Keevil's support enabled me to meet Heinz Schimmelbusch, then the chair of Metallgesellschaft (MG), now CEO of AMG Advanced Metallurgical Group. According to Vladimir Lenin, MG was like a giant octopus and had its fingers in everything. Norman also introduced me to Norman Fussell, CEO of MIM Holdings. The rumour was Teck, MG, and MIM were trying to corner the zinc market. At a road show of Metall Mining, an MG subsidiary, Heinz was asked by someone in the audience what he thought of zinc prices, to which he replied, "What are you doing for dinner tonight?" The packed house could not stop laughing. He was a charming speaker.

Financing junior mining companies had several problems, as it often attracted the wrong kind of people in the nineties, which gave the Vancouver Stock Exchange a bad name, especially after numerous articles appeared in the *New York Times* describing how investors had been ripped off, for lack of a better term. But mining was in my blood, so I tried to associate myself with good mining promoters that found resources and built mines. I spent a long time convincing Nesbitt Thomson to look at mining exploration companies, which were a hard sell in the earlier years. However, we created a mining team and became a major factor in the mining sector.

I also went into mining by necessity, because Canada's junior mining centre is Vancouver and our traditional investment banking business had almost disappeared. One day, Brian Aune and I visited Austin Taylor of McLeod Young Weir to see if we could get a piece of the Westcoast Transmission syndicate. Austin was a big name in BC business; Taylor Way, the road you take in West Vancouver on your way to Whistler, was named after his grandfather, who owned most of the property off it. Westcoast was a big issuer, and it would have helped our BC business, which was quite small. Sadly, we didn't have enough underwriting at the time and were left out of the financing.

—

MOLSON STADIUM, above the city of Montreal up University Avenue, is where McGill played football in 1960. Since the university owned the stadium, I was able to get tickets to almost every game. It was worth it because 1960 was a great year for McGill, which won the national championship led by a quarterback by the name of Tom Skypeck. Earlier in the season, the centre had been injured. Skypeck looked around and asked who was the backup, and someone replied it was a guy called John Cleghorn. Skypeck said, "Make sure he practises and goes home with a bloody nose every day." As everyone who understands football knows, the centre is one of the most important positions for the quarterback—without a good snap, the quarterback cannot implement the play.

A quarter of a century later, in 1985, I was trying to raise money to buy Nesbitt Thomson shares, as Brian Aune was taking the company public and offering a large amount of stock. Brian's long-term goal was to build up the company and sell it to a Canadian bank; but before that happened, he wanted to take the firm public. In that offering, Brian made fifty millionaires; I was one of them.

I knew it was a smart investment, but unfortunately, I had too much debt and was maxed out with RBC. When I went to my banker, Core Dewitt, on the ground floor of the Royal Centre, and told him I needed a million dollars, he replied, "We all need a million dollars." Growing desperate, I asked him if I could go see the man upstairs, the head of RBC in BC, John Cleghorn, a banker I had known in my times as a research analyst in Montreal, when he was president of Mercantile Bank of Canada. I made an appointment to see John, and I told him to call Brian Aune in Montreal and ask how important I was to his organization. A few weeks later, John called me back to his office and told me I had the million dollars I had asked for. I thanked him and said, "I have no idea how I will ever pay you back, but every shareholder bonus I get, I will give it to you."

Unheard of today, the loan had no security, except the shares I was buying; no fixed payment schedule; and a very low interest rate of only prime plus 1 percent. Two years later we went public, and I went to see John again to give him a cheque for $900,000, keeping $100,000 as a loan with RBC. John went on to become the president of RBC and governor emeritus of McGill University. I saw him one last time when he came to Vancouver on his retirement tour. I told Peter Newman this story in front of John, and he said he remembered it like it was yesterday.

Brian completed the process in 1987, selling Nesbitt Thomson to the Bank of Montreal (now BMO); Brian Steck was appointed as president and CEO. The sale was made possible by Canadian government regulatory reforms made that year that broke down the four pillars—banks, trust companies, insurance companies, and broker dealers—and allowed banks to purchase investment houses. The deal was historic, the first time a Canadian chartered bank had bought a Canadian investment firm.

The deal was a $175 million public offering—part secondary, part treasury. Not bad for a guy who couldn't pay his American Express bills in the early seventies.

In the Bank of Montreal's elegant architectural masterpiece in Old Montreal is a museum which features a plaque acknowledging the contributions of three men who figured so prominently in my life: Brian Aune, Brian Steck, and Jacques Ménard.

—

OCCASIONALLY, I took a break from financing mining companies to finance something else, like a ski resort. Anyone who knows me knows that I love skiing. Not the normal alpine skiing but telemark, also known as free skiing or cross-country downhill. I started telemark skiing in Whistler in the early eighties after years of cross-country marathons in BC, Quebec, and the Yukon. In those years, the Canadian Ski Association gave you a bronze pin when you completed three marathons in one year, a silver one if you completed three more the following year, and a gold one if you completed three more in the third year. I still have the gold pin, which I wear occasionally. My passion for skiing in Whistler led me, with another skier, to create the Whistler Telemark Club. The members were a cast of characters, who often showed up at our house, where Chris would feed them a lasagna dinner. They ate as if they hadn't eaten in a week. They came from all walks of life, but were mostly ski bums.

Unlike surfing, I'm actually good at skiing. I learned to do it in the eighties at Whistler Blackcomb, where I took my first lesson with Bob Disbrow, and I was hooked. If a cat has nine lives, a telemark skier has twenty. I learned how to do it with some of the best telemarkers out there when we formed the club.

The original telemark boots were leather and were hooked up on the binding to the ski in three pins (hence the name, three-pin binding). Later I graduated to NTN bindings, which hook up under the boot. The bindings don't release very often, even on high impact. Most telemark skiers wear knee pads for protection when they fall forward, which happened a lot in the old times. An instructor said to me one day, "It's like doing a thousand lunges."

Telemark turns in deep powder are a sight to behold. The arc of the turn is longer than in alpine skiing, which is why this is the only time you can pass an alpine skier. Going down a double black diamond in Whistler called the Diamond Bowl, I was behind Lukas Lundin, who looked up and asked, "How can you ski on those miserable sticks?" Telemark skiing has been called ballet on skis as you counter your weight, pushing the ski and dropping your heel in an elegant forward thrust. I learned to ski with the best. Going down the Saudan Couloir, in the early days we would pop an Advil to dull the sore muscles. I used to go hard all day, skiing in places we shouldn't have.

One day, in a blinding snowstorm on the Couloir, I almost hit an attractive girl from Toronto halfway down the mountain. She told me, "Anyone who can ski down this run on those kind of skis can get as close to me as they like." Another time, I was going down the same run with a fund manager from New York City whose desire was always to ski one day more each year than his age; he was in his late sixties at the time. We proceeded to ski all day with a mining executive named Mike Jones, who said at the end, "You kicked my ass all day."

Sometimes, I would end up in St. Paul's hospital in the ER, waiting my turn to have my knees and legs checked. I never told anyone I was the chair of the foundation; I just sat there and hoped nothing was broken.

Telemark skiing was a way of reducing stress from investment banking and charity work. I had a friend who never liked to ski out on a normal run, so we took the Singing Pass Trailhead back to the village to avoid the crowds. I don't see him anymore, but I miss him.

From November to early May, I still ski at least fifty days a year, which I am fully convinced helps reduce my stress level. The adrenaline rush keeps me coming back year after year.

Back to financing that ski hill. I was an investment banker who loved to ski. This prompted me to call Joe Houssian, who owned the Blackcomb Mountain ski resort and property development company Intrawest. I told him that I'd like to come and see him, with an idea. Charles Addison, an investment banker who worked for me, came to the meeting. I said, "Joe, you should take Intrawest public."

He listened and said, "Should I throw the real estate in too?" We said yes. Joe had just bought Blackcomb Mountain from the federal development bank for $6 million. I told Joe not to worry about Whistler, the ski hill right next to Blackcomb that he did not own: "Once you are public, you will have the currency, and the owner of Whistler Mountain will come to you as they are locked into a private company, and the logical buyer is Intrawest."

That is exactly what happened a few years later. Joe was known as a tough negotiator, but he liked me and gave Nesbitt Thomson the mandate, and said, "You pick the syndicate, and make sure you get this job done." We raised $32 million in 1994. In 2016, Intrawest sold Whistler Blackcomb to Vail Resorts for a value of $1.4 billion Canadian. Ultimately, Intrawest was sold for $1.5 billion to Henry Crown and Company in 2017.

One day after a long day on the slopes, I attended an event at Bishop's restaurant in Vancouver, a showing of Haida artist Robert Davidson's carvings. Several hours earlier in Whistler, I had climbed up a spot called Spanky's Ladder in a blinding snowstorm. This gateway to the high alpine area on Blackcomb Mountain isn't really a ladder, but there are often footprints in the snow from people climbing up it to get to the black and double-black runs up there. I asked the lifty if the entrance to the Blackcomb glacier was open, to which she responded in the affirmative. I started to climb the steep stairs leading to a run entering the valley below. At the top of the wind-blown area, two men from Fernie, BC, who were on a ski trip asked me how to get out of there. I told them to head straight down the valley and keep towards the centre, but for some strange, unknown reason, I did not follow them, and instead followed the ski patrol's tracks to where he had put a stake to warn skiers of the danger below. The problem was that the stake had been blown down, and not knowing that, I suddenly found myself airborne in a narrow chute, somehow landing on an edge thirty feet below.

At that point, I heard the two men from Fernie ask if I was OK, to which I replied, "I think so." Not knowing how far the drop was to safety, I asked them if it was level below. They said it was about twenty feet or so from where I was. I quickly took the drop. When I saw them, they told me, "I thought we were going to have to take you out of here in a body bag," a phrase I had not heard since I left Vietnam.

After buying my rescuers a beer, I drove down to Vancouver and went to the Bishop's. Sitting next to me was Malcom Parry, a well-known society writer for the *Vancouver Sun*, who told me that he wasn't working that night. So, not thinking anything more, I told him the whole story. The next morning, the *Sun* published it in full. I received several calls and emails from my friends saying they would not ski with me anymore.

—

WHISTLER HAS been a part of my life since I moved to Vancouver from Montreal in the eighties. In 2001, I was asked by Shauna Hardy, the founder, to join the board of the Whistler Film Festival (WFF)—not because I knew anything about movies, but because she is a friend and thought I could help. One of my fondest memories of Shauna is waiting for the ski patrollers to open the alpine area at Spanky's Ladder. Shauna pulled out her sandwich, and so did I as we waited. We munched away happily together, thinking about Diamond Bowl, Sapphire Bowl, and Ruby Bowl below, all of which involve treacherous terrain if you do not know the area well.

Other than the Toronto film festival, WFF is the only film festival in Canada supported by *Variety*, the Los Angeles–based magazine founded in 1905 that is one of the leading publications of the movie industry. At the festival I met Steven Gaydos, an executive VP of *Variety*, who has written a couple books but is best known as the writer and producer of the 2010 film *Road to Nowhere*. I sponsored numerous dinners at the festival and got to know Steven pretty well. Today he is responsible for 250 publications a year for *Variety*. Steven loves WFF. He introduced me to Phil Keith, who was a Marine in Vietnam as I was. I had a fundraising event at my house in West Vancouver, which raised a lot of money for the WFF, as many of my friends bought some excellent art pieces.

One day, when I was about to go down Saudan Couloir on Blackcomb, I saw a skier make the sign of the cross before he headed down the run and heard him tell his buddy that if something happened to tell his wife he loved her. I found his comments a bit dramatic, yet if I had thought about it a little longer I may have agreed with him and not gone down that run at all. You have to be up to it to do double-black runs like that with deep moguls and no way out, especially on telemark skis.

Shortly after we took Blackcomb public through Intrawest in 1994, I met Mei McCurdy, now Mei Madden, a beautiful young woman working at the time for Intrawest, who told me about the Founders Pass for Whistler Blackcomb. One thing led to another, and I ended up purchasing the pass and contributing to the Whistler Blackcomb Foundation and becoming one of the original sponsors. The foundation gives out millions of dollars a year, and I am still a member of the Founders Club. Each year Whistler gives out fifty passes, which allow you to get to the front of the line and take three guests up with you for one time only. The cost of $6,500 today may not be a bargain, but the revenue has supported the Whistler Blackcomb Foundation for almost thirty years. Although I do from time to time consider not renewing it, I couldn't do that to Mei. I hear that there is a waitlist of ten years for this pass.

13

GAME CHANGER

It's Always about People

I N THE SUMMER of 1994, I had just arrived at my place in Tofino when I was told to head back to Vancouver and then to Toronto, where we were to meet with the CEO of BMO, Matt Barrett, on the top floor of First Canadian Place. It turned out that the bank had just acquired Burns Fry Ltd to create a larger investment banking firm, Nesbitt Burns, to give BMO more presence in Toronto to go along with our presence in Montreal. By then the bank had spent half a billion dollars on brokerage firms, and they assured us that nothing would change and no one would get laid off, but I did not believe a word of it. BMO had just broken down the four pillars, and they were about to become bigger.

At the BMO head office on Place d'Armes in Montreal, there is a small Bank of Montreal Museum. A few years ago, I visited it on a private tour arranged for me by Jacques Ménard, an old friend who was then the CEO of BMO Nesbitt Burns Quebec. On the plaques were the names of Brian Aune and Brian Steck, both friends of mine in different ways. Being a student of history, it was astonishing to me how this bank had grown from a small business on Rue Saint-Paul—Canada's first bank, where much of the history of the country started—to the huge BMO it is today.

I decided to leave, not because I wasn't making enough money, but because I felt the writing was on the wall, and everything would change in the transition from a small employee-owned firm to a global bank. I decided that I would start my own brokerage firm with Alan Herrington, who had been let go from Nesbitt Thomson when they acquired Burns Fry. I had spent twenty-one years at Nesbitt Thomson, and it was time for a change. I had done as much as I could at the firm, most of my friends had either been terminated or moved on, and my new role would have been to become partners with people who had been my competitors. Moreover, with my friend Brian Aune gone (he had stepped down as CEO in 1990), I faced the prospect of being a glad-hander with a much-reduced role in a much larger bank setting. Most importantly, I would go from reporting to two people to reporting to many.

Sadly, my last job at Nesbitt Thomson was to fire employees I had hired. So, one by one, I negotiated with each terminated employee the bank's severance package. One day after all the employees had been terminated, my assistant Martine and I went to Bishop's restaurant to try to forget what we had been through. As we sat there about to have our dinner, Ken Shields, the president of another brokerage firm, Goepel Shields & Partners, sent over an expensive bottle of wine. We continued to have a first-class meal with no shortage of sadness. The tough business of investment banking was not about to get any easier.

Salman Partners was born with the help of Neil de Gelder, who was senior counsel at Borden Ladner Gervais LLP at the time. To start with, we were homeless, with no proper office. So we set about trying to find a space and do some basic things like open a business phone line, which I found out was almost impossible unless you had a previous business account.

My whole life I have struggled with the fear of the unknown, from joining the Marines to moving across the country. My mother's profound faith taught me to reach for higher goals and to never give up when the going gets tough. The comfort of BMO—a large expense account, an extensive travel budget, and the prestige of being their only executive VP west of Toronto—was a hard thing to let go. Operating from my desk at St. Paul's Hospital (where I was chair of the foundation; more on that later), I tried to open a bank account and find office space to accommodate the new firm and our six employees. On the eighth floor of One Bentall Centre in downtown Vancouver, with borrowed furniture and a bunch of phone lines, we started Salman Partners. The original six were my daughter Krista, the receptionist and jack of all trades, who had just graduated from McGill and spent the winter skiing at Whistler; Bill Burk, the head trader, who had just been let go by Burns after arriving in Vancouver; Sam Magid, who had worked at Nesbitt Thomson as a salesman and was our new head of institutional equity; Ian Todd, our CFO, who came from member services at the Vancouver Stock Exchange; Alan Herrington; and me.

Why would anyone want to start a brokerage firm? Ego or a dream to be like everyone else at the research department at Nesbitt Thomson twenty years earlier. It was not about greed, but a desire to build something special with the skills I had. It was still an age where people paid for ideas, and the power of the ideas mattered.

In a business which often has low integrity, we were determined to build something special, something with high integrity. The camaraderie that came with a small firm where everyone shared the same vision created the best teamwork I've ever seen outside the Marines. The former president of Salomon Brothers in

New York once said, "Investment banking is the art of moving people to action." At Salman Partners, we did that in spades. On one of those early days, as we were struggling to grow the business, we received a sizable cheque by mistake in the mail, with the name Salomon Brothers on it. We laughed at the irony—we could have used the money.

I asked Norm Keevil of Teck Resources if he would like to be a shareholder of Salman Partners, to which he said, "I could help more if I wasn't a shareholder." Shortly thereafter, Norm asked me if I could recommend a potential director for Teck. I thought about it for a while and told him that Brian Aune would be a good one. Years later, after Brian had been on the board for many years, Norm told me that he was the best director they had. I went to numerous mine openings with Teck over the years, including Hemlo in Northern Ontario and the Bullmoose coal mine in British Columbia.

Sam Magid was the best institutional salesman I've ever worked with, and I've worked with many. One early morning, he called me on my home phone. He said, "I know what you are doing, and I am going to join you and I'll have a cappuccino ready for you in the office." Sam could convince the most skeptical fund manager of the merits of an investment. In those days, none of us took a salary, and none of us had a contract. We decided who got what based on merit, and we always made sure we had some left over for our administrative staff.

Sam could sell anything he believed in. I always knew that he would flatten our inventory positions every day. Sam was a very good forestry analyst, and at one point was ranked by StarMine, a ranking service which grades investment analysts. One day in the fall of 1994, fund manager John Priestman asked Sam for his model for a company called Pacific Logging, which was owned by Canadian Pacific. Falling back on his chair, Sam replied, "It's just coming off the printer." This wasn't literally true, but the model had been in Sam's mind on a computer, sort of. He scrambled to produce a full-blown research report to send John.

We were eight people by October, so it took us a while, but we had the ability to turn around a research report very quickly. We improvised where we could, always managed to work up first-class research, and never had a client complain about our product. Sam's idea was to market forestry companies that owned private timber lands as opposed to Crown land, as private land was more valuable. Fund managers loved the distinction because private land had the ability to increase in value. Sam ran the institution like a drill instructor. Everyone reported to him, and he would not have had it any other way, because he was dealing with the firm's capital, something we did not have much of.

Sam was my partner for thirteen years. He eventually left because his intense personality had the potential to cause him and the firm more difficulties in the long run. We reluctantly decided to part—it was especially difficult as his heart was always in the right place and he wore the Salman Partners logo on his shirt. His hard work and dedication allowed me to give back so much in so many ways, notably with St. Paul's Hospital and the Vancouver Public Library Foundation. He simply said to me, "Kahuna, I want you to do your charity work, and don't worry if something comes up, I will take care of it."

After Sam left Salman Partners, he said he was not going any-where, but he was. He moved to Beverly Hills, California, where he became enormously wealthy and lived in a $20 million man-sion. He was rumoured to be involved with many famous actresses, including Lindsay Lohan, who was even investigated after his luxury watch collection was stolen. He loved watches. Several years ago, his housekeeper found him dead, alone in his mansion, at the age of fifty-two.

I spoke at his funeral in Vancouver. I recall that I remembered him as a trustworthy partner and a deeply caring person. Then I quoted Dietrich Bonhoeffer, something along the lines of, "This life was not the grand finale, the next one is." As I said to those in attendance, "Sam would like that option."

Life at One Bentall was simple. None of us took salaries in the early days. We were paid from the institutional and industrial banking pools. When we travelled, we flew economy and stayed at friends' houses when we could, which was often the case in Montreal, Toronto, and a few other cities, such as New York, Boston, and Chicago. We often took red-eye flights so we did not have to pay for a hotel. We had no art on the office walls except some paintings my wife had when she was in Toronto and single. The rental furniture worked out well, and the trading desk was the size of a normal dining room table, except it was oval.

Our seventh employee was Haytham Hodaly, whom I hired as a mining analyst. I got his name from John Meeks, who had been a student of my father's at McGill. One day I called John and asked him if he had a student who could become the main mining analyst at our firm. He introduced me to Haytham, who he thought would be a good candidate, not only because he was a mining engineer, but also because he was pursuing a master's degree in mineral economics at UBC at the time. I called Haytham and asked if he was interested in the position, to which he responded, "I would like to talk to you about it."

So we met, and Haytham said, "I would like to help, but I am working on my master's degree and also have a part-time job." We ultimately reached an agreement where he would work as our mining analyst part-time until he finished his degree. I told him this suited us because I could only afford to pay him a part-time salary anyway. We drew up a one-page contract that outlined his salary and potential opportunities to participate in the company's bonus pool. I made him put on every research report that he was a candidate for a master's and had completed all the course work, but was yet to be awarded the degree. He hated that title—"Master's candidate." So, we had an analyst, and could be considered serious in the mining business. No one knew that Haytham only worked part-time, or that he was also working as a private investigator to pay the bills, or about his impressive resumé, which included a black belt in karate.

Often when I called Haytham to talk about various mining projects or the companies we were going to cover, he would tell me to hold on for a minute because he was on an investigation, acting for a client or a disgruntled spouse to find out what their partners were up to. I always imagined he was hiding behind a pillar or some other obstruction while he tailed the subject his firm was investigating. Meanwhile I was trying to explain to him that we needed to look at this silver company, as we had a meeting coming up.

I remember one time when Haytham published a research report on a mining company called Kinross Gold. After reading it, the *Wall Street Journal* picked Kinross as the number one performing stock that year, which prompted a fund manager in New York City by the name of John Paulson to buy millions of shares of Kinross, paying us seven cents a share along the way. Today that commission would be one cent a share, if you were lucky.

Haytham went on to cover the largest precious metal companies in the world, including Barrick, Silver Wheaton, Silver Standard, Yamana Gold, Pan American Silver, and a number of others. He also worked as co-director of research. Our approach to mining research was simple—follow good companies with good geology and experienced people with known track records.

Haytham became the best producer of mining financial models, which provided us with first-class research. His models were more detailed than most, and each mine had its own model, which was rare. We treated his research reports as pieces of art and used the financial models as the cores around which we built our recommendations.

We built our brokerage firm on an individual basis and strived to produce only the facts along with our recommendations. In all the years of Salman Partners, we never had a client complaint, which is almost unheard of today. We paid lower salaries than other, bigger companies because that was all we could afford, but we offered our employees equity that would grow for years afterwards. We tried to avoid people who were prima donnas and hired from the best universities and those with CFAs and MBAs. We knew full well that over time we would lose people because, we learned early on, our competitors did not like to train people.

During the early days I received a call from Brett Wilson, who's famous for *Dragons' Den*. He came to Vancouver to discuss the possibility of merging First Energy and Salman Partners. It was an idea I regret not exploring as it would have created a mining and energy powerhouse based out of Western Canada.

One of the more interesting hires I made was Nicholas Campbell, the son of the former BC premier Gordon Campbell. Nicholas called me from Victoria and said he wanted to visit me for a potential job interview. After sitting at our boardroom table and listening to the Salman Partners story up to that point in time, Nicholas said to me, "OK, but I'm not sure that I want to join the investment business because of the low moral integrity of the industry." After I took a deep breath, I said, "I agree with you, but you can be an exception." After another ten minutes of discussion, I wished him well and told him to call me should he change his mind. A few months later, I received a call from Nicholas, and he joined Salman Partners as a research associate working for Haytham.

At Salman Partners, we could compete because we were going downstream to finance junior companies (because that was where the growth was) as well as a few larger ones. There were many opportunities, and we were very creative, but we did not have the capital of the large banks. We were able to convince issuers to deal with this. For example, once we convinced West Fraser Timber to complete a private placement of $40 million worth of their common equity. The buyer, Phillips, Hager & North, wanted the shares and was willing to accept the four-month hold, and the issuer, West Fraser, liked the price and commission savings vis-à-vis a more expensive bought deal. We also had the benefit of what was called a bank letter, which enabled us to double our capital with a credit facility from one of the major banks. Unfortunately, this came to an end a few years later because the regulators considered these types of letters off-balance-sheet financing by the banks.

Hank Ketcham and his son Pete of West Fraser were both our clients and early shareholders of Salman Partners. They rarely wore ties, and we were part of the syndicate that took them public. Sam Magid provided the forestry research, and I was CEO and co-director of research. At one annual meeting of West Fraser in the company's hometown of Quesnel, BC, Hank gave me his US draft card in a frame with a note that had "Thanks, Terry" stamped across it, because I went to Vietnam and he did not. West Fraser went on to become the largest lumber producer in the world, with a market cap today of $5.58 billion.

During my twenty-five years at Salman Partners, I was CEO and either director or co-director of research. We financed hundreds of companies, but I never forgot my research background. One day from that humble office on the eighth floor of One Bentall, I saw several buy-and-sell tickets on the floor that a fund manager of Gluskin Sheff had given us for an introduction we had made to David Radler, then a partner of Conrad Black. These trades paid the bills at a time when we had little revenue. SP traded in the Vancouver Stock Exchange because we had yet to have a seat in

Toronto. The value of our trades (ticket size) was often the largest on the VSE, as we did largely institutional businesses. The VSE stayed open half an hour after the TSE (now the TSX) closed. One day, we gave a large sell order of an owner of CP shares, which we crossed on the VSE after the TSE had closed. In the years of One Bentall, we had no revenue, no clients, and little capital, but over time we grew to nearly a hundred people with big ideas and big dreams. Our research was among the best anywhere and sought after by investors globally.

As at Salman Partners, a lot of pride went into the research we produced. We were a mining research house, and many people relied on our research product, though ironically a fair amount of them did not pay for it. We were the first to make big calls on copper, and we were the first company to research First Quantum Minerals, which today has a market capital of $14 billion. Another company we covered was Nevsun Resources, which was sold to Zijin Mining Group for $1.8 billion in 2018. We picked sectors and companies that were not in favour or were up-and-comers, which ultimately provided multiple returns to our clients.

Salman Partners was an idea that everyone bought into, except for a few West Coast–based institutions. Our support came from global institutions, particularly ones based in the US. In addition to our research, our support came from a significant number of junior mining companies that we researched. One US fund manager told us we gave him the same or better-quality research than CIBC, even though, he knew, we were much smaller. We did hundreds of transactions, supported for the most part by our own independent research, either written or verbal. Our integrity was based on the value of our research opinions, never by investment banking. One day I received two phone calls from two executives, the CEO and the chair, of the same mining company complaining about our analysts' view of energy costs in Chile. I listened but stood by our research.

Salman Partners' growth enabled me to give back more. Each month we were successful, I made a point of making time for working with the various charities I was getting involved with, starting with St. Paul's Hospital. Going up to the hospital was a break that allowed me to get away from the focus on making money, paying bonuses, and listening to people complaining about not making enough. When we had our best years, and when we didn't, I continued to give back through the hospital.

Salman Partners was a huge success—we were at the right place at the right time. The institutional work was what kept the lights on, with salaries, TSE fees, and all the other miscellaneous costs of running an investment business. Corporate finance business enabled us to pay bonuses and build our capital base. The institutions paid for our research, and the corporate finance part was gravy—and so successful were we at the time that the Canadian regulators gave us a risk profile that was comparable to those of the Canadian chartered banks. The larger institutions in the US would pay up to seven cents per share for a trade. One year, the *Wall Street Journal* wrote that Salman Partners provided the highest returns of any stocks on their list that year in their review of research recommendations. Our analyst Haytham Hodaly made the right call on Kinross and First Quantum.

But changes were on the way. In addition to the cancellation of bank letters, which had given smaller dealers a competitive edge, a secondary condition was a best practice requirement that forced institutions to offer the best practice on the trade, essentially meaning that only a bank could provide the best price. This had the effect of eliminating small dealers' abilities to compete. It was a very poor argument, and it changed the landscape forever.

—

IN MY office in Vancouver is a cartoon drawing of the members of the Expert Panel on Securities Regulation in Canada that was given to me by Jim Flaherty, Canada's minister of finance, in 2008. He signed it, "In appreciation of your dedication and advice." The first time David Murchison, who then worked in the department and was the minister's chief liaison with the panel members, approached me and asked me to serve on it, I refused. It was 2008, and I was worried about the impact the financial crisis would have on smaller firms such as Salman Partners. We had almost a hundred employees, and running the business was costing us around $200,000 a month. So reluctantly, I said no to David. One of the few times I ever refused an honourable request.

So, I returned to work, trying to reduce costs and being forced to cut staff. I was worried. A few months later, however, David approached me again and added, "The minister really wants you to do this." After taking a deep breath, I said, "David, if the minister really wants me to, I cannot say no." In more than thirty years in the investment business, I had met many finance ministers in Canada, and in my opinion, Jim Flaherty was the best (followed by Paul Martin and Joe Oliver). He was almost single-handedly the reason Canada escaped the financial crisis in 2008 relatively unscathed. Jim Flaherty was more than a finance minister. He was revered by his colleagues and other global finance ministers. He truly cared about this country, and his integrity was beyond question. When I first met him in his office in Ottawa, I was impressed with how genuine he was. His commitment to Canada and his desire to put himself above politics made me admire him even more. He had a keen mind and a sense of humour; no wonder he was awarded a state funeral by Prime Minister Harper in 2014.

Sitting on the expert panel was many hours of work as we set out to make the case for a national securities commission, a regulatory body that has eluded Canada for years, making us one of the only major industrial countries without one. My most significant contribution was to support the role of small business and create an agency that would recognize and support them, as small business is where the most jobs are created in Canada. While there wasn't political will to create a national commission, many provinces took up the cause by lowering the threshold to financing for junior companies.

—

SALMAN PARTNERS continued to be a success in the mid-nineties and up to mid-2005, due to our ability to make people essential returns. Between 1994 and 2000, we opened offices in Toronto and Calgary. We generally hired people from Queen's, McGill, UBC, and the Fletcher School at Tufts in Boston, where my daughter Krista had graduated. For the most part, we had an open-plan office to encourage our staff to engage in open dialogue whenever possible. There was a probation period with a basic salary and a right to participate in the bonus pool, but not much else. The business was driven by people's desire to make money. The idea was a partnership that emphasized teamwork and the feeling of belonging to grow a successful business. It was the people I liked about the business, and the opportunities we created for individuals to realize their potential. I would spend hours talking to the lowest-level employees, listening to any big ideas they might have.

In the early days, we enjoyed a close working relationship with all the employees of Salman Partners. We went on retreats and various trips together to build team morale. We also had dinners and drinks after work and engaged in other fun team-building activities.

I was big on loyalty as, after all, I am a Marine. Sadly, the investment industry lacks loyalty, but there are exceptions—and that was why Salman Partners was successful. Haytham, for instance, was one of our long-term, loyal employees—he spent almost fifteen years with us before reluctantly moving to RBC. He went on to become senior VP of Wheaton Precious Metals, one of the world's largest precious metal streaming companies and a long-standing client of Salman Partners to this day.

Tori Fahey was a twenty-one-year-old finance graduate from the University of Calgary working on her CFA when I hired her. She produced more research reports in one year than any other analyst in the history of Salman Partners. When I told her I needed a website, she responded, "I can do that for you, just buy me a home computer." After a number of years with Salman Partners, she left the firm to be a founding partner of KERN Partners and ultimately cashed out to create Apidura, a bike-packing company that gave people the opportunity to travel by bicycle to places rarely reached by others. Today they produce a range of bike-packing gear that gets high reviews. She completed her MBA with INSEAD in Singapore and Paris and cycled through many countries across Africa, Europe, and America. We share the same birthday and are still friends to this day. I have missed her since the day she left Salman Partners.

Frank Mele was a lawyer whom I hired as a banker in our Calgary office to work on oil and gas transactions. We worked together for eight years, and he was a true partner, especially during the Newport Petroleum bought deal, which went bad when the company was sued by another oil and gas executive. We had a bank letter that enabled us to buy this deal along with Peters & Co. and TD. The problem was Peters & Co.'s lead manager refused to request the company reprice this deal. We lost about half our capital in this transaction, and I, with the Royal Bank, managed the liquidation of the position. Frank Mele and I and Sam put up more capital when we had no choice. When Frank asked me how important it was to the firm, he insisted on riding with me to the airport in a taxi to hear my answer. Other shareholders were getting nervous during this fiasco, and two founding shareholders sold their positions back to us; one was Ron Shon, whose family owned a portion of the Cathedral Place in Vancouver; the other was Mo Farris, who once told me that "getting out of an interest in a private company is like trying to get out of a Catholic marriage." Frank continued to be my partner until he left to become a successful oil and gas fund manager with KERN Partners in Calgary.

From 1994 to 2015, Salman Partners was a highly profitable firm for the most part. We grew our capital base year after year after paying out bonuses and dividends. In early 2001, the Toronto Stock Exchange (TSX) Group was formed following TSE's acquisition of Canadian Venture Exchange. It was a big win for the industry, as we were shareholders of the TSX at the time. Our strategy was to give the proceeds of these shares to our shareholders based on the percentage of their ownership of Salman Partners, a move that prompted one shareholder to send me a unique gift.

A rodeo silver belt buckle is a thing of beauty, especially one made by one of the top silversmiths in the United States. David Radler, one of our more colourful shareholders at the time, had this belt buckle fashioned with my name on it on a silver background with a gold braid wrapped around it. It was produced by Montana Silversmiths of Columbus, Montana, and David gave it to me to wear to the Calgary Stampede. It was as unique of a present as you can get, a thank-you gift for his proceeds and percentage interest in the TSX shares.

14

A HOSPITAL
SECOND TO NONE

I NEVER WENT INTO investment banking to make money. It just somehow happened that way. At university, I learned finance but played with the idea of being a journalist or a gym instructor, or maybe working for a non-profit. At one point, as I was struggling with the aftermath of the Vietnam War, I even considered joining the Anglican priesthood. I only stumbled into investment banking while looking for a part-time job to feed my family while I pursued my MBA. In the end, I love the game, but not the greed. More than anything else, the money I earned gave me the ability to give back.

My first adventure in giving back began with a chance encounter with Linda Dickson, the charismatic executive director of St. Paul's Hospital Foundation. She was a very attractive woman, who had been married to Peter Dickson, the son of a former chief justice of Canada. And she had all the qualities of a born leader. Over lunch one day in 1988, Linda convinced me to join the board of the foundation. She was hard to say no to. Everyone I spoke to in those days loved her—the medical staff, the board, and most importantly, the donors, people like Tong Louie, founder of HY Louie and London Drugs.

Linda had earned her MBA in a time when most women did not. She was fiercely independent and believed that women should make it on their own and not depend on men. Raising money for the hospital was tough work, but Linda made it seem like fun and never stopped trying. The memory of seeing her smile in her office off the main entrance of the hospital, where the foundation was located, is still with me.

I could walk away from investment banking any day, but one trader had the ability to put the firm under, so I was always under stress. No one was too big to fail, and small players like us were expendable, especially as the regulators never cut us much slack. I was Salman Partners' UDP (ultimate designated person) in Canada and the US, a title that always frightened me. But from the moment I joined the St. Paul's board, I would go and sit in Linda's office and put any problems I had behind me. She made me a better chairman, who would never take no for an answer, and we reached for the moon. She used to say, "We can do this Terry," and I always looked at her smiling face and replied, "Yes, we can."

The idea was to increase St. Paul's presence in the fundraising circle. It all started with Linda, who worked non-stop; in her mind, the hospital could do no wrong. I spoke to her almost every day when I was in Vancouver and sometimes when I was travelling abroad. She was a fundraiser asking for money as most fundraisers do, but Linda had a way of making you feel good about it. I never tired of helping her and took it as just a good thing to do. We were giving back, and she always took criticism with grace and reflection. She always made me feel that I was doing something important, and in the big scheme of things, she was right. Linda constantly searched for new ways to look after the needs of the hospital—she did it in spades, and I jumped on the bandwagon.

One day we found out from the medical staff that we needed our first MRI machine. We received a commitment from the government to aid in funding the purchase of the equipment and decided to offer them a deal; we would raise half the money if they would match our contribution. I love sharing deals, and so do governments.

The hardest thing to raise money for at any hospital is research, and Linda and I took this as a challenge. She made fundraising interesting, and we pushed each other to get more done.

After I founded Salman Partners, once a week or so, I'd walk up to St. Paul's to have a meeting with Linda. In those days, the foundation was right in the middle of the hospital where all the action was, by the entrance on Burrard Street. The hospital had no security staff at the entrance to the emergency department until the Vancouver Police Department got us to hire our own security. At one board meeting we presented all the weapons that had been confiscated from visitors to the ER, including machetes, knives, and handguns. If someone who was involved in a drug trade was being treated in emergency, they were sometimes attacked by a rival gang member.

I was not the only one who visited Linda at her office often. Tong Louie was chairman emeritus when I was chair. He used to visit Linda at the foundation after his daily workout at the YMCA, next door to the hospital. We rarely talked about business, but always talked about hospitals. One day, he and I took a walk to the Hotel Vancouver, where he convinced the managers to donate a breakfast to the foundation. He also convinced the news anchor of CBC at the time, Knowlton Nash, to come and speak about national affairs at the breakfast. We filled the room with paying business clients and created another source of revenue for the foundation. Another time, Tong convinced Ted Rogers, president of Rogers Communications, to come to speak at a corporate breakfast; behind my desk is a picture of me giving Ted a framed photo of St. Paul's Hospital.

While I was chair of the St. Paul's Hospital Foundation, we accomplished several notable achievements. The most significant was starting Canada's first hospital lottery, an idea that came from Tony Petrina, who was the CEO of Placer Dome, one of the world's largest gold producers, at the time and one of our board members. Starting in 1990, we ran this lottery with our own staff, and for the eight years I was chair, it was our most successful single source of revenue. The first prize was a condominium in Vancouver, and for several years our revenue exceeded $2 million a year, net of the price of the condo. But a lottery like this is risky; if we couldn't sell enough tickets to pay for the condo, the foundation would have been on the hook. But I never let that happen. We had dedicated staff who only dealt with lotteries and a list of condo ticket buyers that grew year by year. We also made sure that we didn't pay too much for the condo and that we negotiated a discounted price with the developers. We also picked the best locations in the downtown Vancouver market. Because of all this, we never lost a nickel on any condo. The foundation staff went into high gear every year once the condo had been purchased. Although the rules changed after some charities lost money on condos while trying to copy us, we never lost money because we managed the process so well.

In my home in West Vancouver, I have a framed photo of all the lottery staff that worked on the project outside the hospital on Burrard Street. It is a reminder of the camaraderie we built in those early days. We didn't stop at condos; we had other lotteries for cars, and even a raffle on a Harley-Davidson motorcycle. The idea in those early days was to increase awareness of the hospital and its needs. St. Paul's Hospital was well known as an institution, but it had never raised money publicly.

Meanwhile, I decided to build out the St. Paul's Hospital Foundation board with prominent businessmen, like Tony Petrina, CEO of Placer; Hank Ketcham, president of West Fraser; David Radler, Conrad Black's business partner at the time; and Peter Newman, who wrote books on the Canadian establishment. I felt that if we were going to raise money for the capital campaign of a hundred-year-old hospital, we needed as many influential people as possible to increase awareness. In those days, there was a feeling that capital should be funded by Catholic organizations. The Sisters of Providence, the Catholic organization that founded St. Paul's, still technically owned the place, and a few of the sisters still lived in the hospital. But all the funding for operations came from the provincial government.

Year after year we pushed a new agenda, with initiatives like the Lights of Hope, which originally raised $50,000 and now raises millions of dollars annually. Linda called me one day and told me that we needed to get on the phone with an organization called Unique Lives in Toronto. They were a fundraising entity that put together events with first-class female speakers and would sell tickets to raise money. We made a deal with them on the phone where we would split the revenue of a fundraiser fifty-fifty. In my office is a picture of me with Lauren Bacall, the legendary actress who was married to Humphrey Bogart and starred with him in classic films like *The Big Sleep* and *Key Largo*. I enjoyed talking to her before I introduced her to a packed house at the Orpheum Theatre in Vancouver. Malcolm Parry took the photo, but when I asked him a few years ago if he had a copy, he said he didn't. Not too long after, he sent me a digital copy in an email that simply read, "Merry Christmas from Lauren Bacall."

Another significant accomplishment was raising money for AIDS research and treatment. As soon as I became chair in 1990, we started to see a wave of AIDS patients at the hospital; by 1993, the hospital was overwhelmed with patients, who largely came from the neighbouring West End or Downtown Eastside. Soon they were dying in record numbers. People were fearful of getting AIDS, and there were all kinds of misconceptions of how you could get it. It was considered a gay man's disease back then. So, we tried to increase awareness of the problem.

I remember taking business leader Jim Pattison through an empty wing of the hospital. It was dark and poorly lit, and there was an eerie silence. He asked me, "Why should I donate money if the rooms are empty?" I said to him, "This is going to be the palliative care unit for AIDS patients. Their last apartment in life. They will be able to take their plants and pets here until they pass away." From then on, he understood. The $600,000 he donated then was a small amount compared to his recent pledge to the new St. Paul's Hospital for seventy-five million, but he made it clear that none of the new pledges would go to the old St. Paul's Hospital.

A year or two later, the palliative care floor was colourful and people seemed happy; even the staff seemed relaxed. It was not restricted access like most other departments in the hospital—entry was easy. The place felt more like an open-plan apartment building than a hospital, which was the aim. I remember talking to many people on this floor and listening to their stories. That was AIDS in the nineties, and we were all learning and adjusting. There was a lot of love on this floor, and you could feel it. Linda and I cringed when ambulance drivers took AIDS patients to other hospitals around town only to be redirected to St. Paul's, the only place they were accepted in those days. In retrospect it was a blessing as we were on to something much bigger.

One of our key goals was to raise money to create the first AIDS chair under Dr. Julio Montaner, who became one of the most successful AIDS practitioners in the world and the head of BC Centre for Excellence in HIV/AIDS, the leading facility of its kind in Canada and recognized globally. It is always harder to raise money for research; donors prefer bricks and mortar. But Dr. Montaner made such an impression on Linda Dickson and me that we persevered. We raised half a million dollars initially, an amount the government of British Columbia agreed to match. I kept the money in our bank account until Premier Mike Harcourt sent Minister of Health Joy MacPhail to the hospital to announce its renewed commitment to St. Paul's. At the same time, we received the government's matching funds for the HIV chair.

The Sisters of Providence supported me in raising funds for AIDS research and palliative care when I was having a difficult time with some board members, who considered it a gay men's disease and "not what we are supposed to be doing." After one of these frustrating conversations, I remember asking David Radler, "If we don't do this, who will?" In the end it didn't matter because the hospital staff and a Roman Catholic nun by the name of Sister Celestine, who was on our board, supported Dr. Montaner and his groundbreaking work.

We also had a group of prominent women who created the Think AIDS Society, which raised money for us and put the issue front and centre. They included Isabel Diamond and Anny Ferman, with support from the CBC commentator Gloria Macarenko. They loved Dr. Montaner, whose work was starting to be recognized internationally, which made my job so much easier. I have a limited-edition Tiko Kerr print that Dr. Montaner recently gave me, entitled "The Halls of Healing (St. Paul's Hospital)," which reminds me of the struggles these artists went through in those days. Gay men were not allowed in the Marine Corps when I was in the service. As an NCO, I was supposed to report cases of homosexuality if I encountered them, but I chose to tell the men in question to refrain from such practices rather than report them. They were good Marines, and it was a different time; I was not about to end their careers and possibly their lives over that. I have a picture in my house of myself with Tong Louie and astronaut Roberta Bondar at one of the razzmatazz fundraising events the Think AIDS women put on. These women were brave and inspired all of us to give more to support Dr. Montaner in his research.

One day, I was taking a train from Greenwich, Connecticut, to New York City and found myself sitting next to a lady who was working away on her laptop. It turned out she was an AIDS researcher who knew Dr. Montaner, who she thought should probably be nominated for a Nobel Prize. This showed us all how St. Paul's Hospital was becoming a world-class research institution, even if most people didn't know it.

After we raised the first million dollars, Dr. Montaner became very successful at raising funds in his own right. He went on to receive both the Order of Canada and the Order of British Columbia. Under his initiative, I became a director of the 625 Powell Street Foundation, a charitable institution funded by a generous donor, Carl Vanderspek. The 625 Powell organization began as a public foundation that provided care for patients of Dr. Montaner and his colleagues in the Downtown Eastside, a sort of a one-stop shop for patients who could not take the long trek to a hospital. I started this work in 1989. From humble beginnings, it grew like the biblical story of the mustard seed.

—

IN 1997, three years after I started Salman Partners, I resigned as chair of St. Paul's Hospital Foundation after eight years in the role. What a run it had been. We had accomplished so much and put the hospital on the map as a foundation.

On February 26, 1997, I received a thoughtful letter signed by Sister Betty Kaczmarczyk, president of the Sisters of Providence.

It read in part, "On behalf of the Sisters of Providence, I wish to thank you for the years of service you have given to St Paul's Hospital Foundation. We appreciate the time, energy and expertise you have given raising funds for the hospital. Your commitment and dedication will not be forgotten. I ask God to bless you abundantly, and you are remembered in our prayers."

After I left the board in 1997, I did not see much of Linda, who also left the board shortly thereafter to join Orca Bay Sports & Entertainment (now Canucks Sports & Entertainment, the company that owns and operates the Vancouver NHL team). She had many jobs after that and always asked me to be a reference; sometimes it was another health-care facility or something similar, but each time I spoke with much fondness for her and her skills. She later moved to Halifax to take care of her aging parents. One day, years later, I saw her by chance on the street in Yaletown. I was very surprised and gave her a big hug. We agreed to meet again but never did; one day, the former director of the foundation called me and told me that Linda had passed away. I was very sad when I heard this. I wish I had kept in touch with her; it was just that I was so busy travelling around the world and doing deals at the peak of the Salman Partners' growth.

Together, Linda and I took giving back to St. Paul's Hospital to a new height. Her death was the end of a remarkable journey with a hundred-year-old institution that did not have much recognition in the fundraising circle when we started. Interestingly, many of the foundation staff who worked for us in those years remained in fundraising. I have a picture of all these women that sits in my house in West Vancouver as a reminder of everything we accomplished.

The Marines taught me to never give up... just find new ways of achieving the same goals. St Paul's Hospital is now a powerhouse fundraising organization. Our efforts put it on the map and laid a path for the future. In our eight years together, Linda and I helped create the first Centre for Excellence in HIV/AIDS, raised funds for the hospital's first MRI machine and the province's first heart centre (named after Tong Louie), and grew the foundation's Lights of Hope. Not a bad step for a hospital the Sisters of Providence started a century ago and one that the people still love.

—

MARINE CORPS Recon teaches Marines how to survive on plants and snakes if necessary. Getting by with less is something the Marines pride themselves on. For me, being frugal started a long time before that. When I was growing up, there was not much money to go around. Each of us had one pair of shoes, and one of everything that we needed. This has always allowed me to keep things in perspective.

Asking people for money is not something my wife, Chris, enjoys. For me, I just look at it as the right thing to do. It doesn't really matter if you get turned down—just keep trying. I started to see it as my way of helping people in need while opening my life up to the possibilities of not focusing on myself so much. In the book *The Second Mountain: The Quest for a Moral Life*, David Brooks talks about life-changing moments as he moves to a higher purpose. By the time I had done ten years of charity work giving back, I was already thinking about my higher purpose.

So much of charity work is spent behind the scenes trying to figure out the best way to move forward; the endless board meetings and tedious community meetings never get much glory in fundraising. But it is this time-consuming work that enables you to get the glory later, maybe. Big donors are hard to come by, and even though you contact many people with much money, it is a well-known fact that those with the least money give the most. People give because they like the fame, but wealthy donors rarely give the first time around. It often takes years of presenting the charity to potential donors before you strike it lucky; the success ratio is probably one in ten. With St. Paul's and the Vancouver Public Library, I tried to get people to buy into the idea, but it was never easy. People would tell me that they were leaving money to their kids more often than not, but sometimes a bright light like Jimmy Pattison or Tong Louie would give not once but twice, or even three times, and it made all the struggle worthwhile.

The world is full of tragic stories and suffering people. So, for those of us who have the opportunity to give back, it just seems like the moral thing to do. It was never just about money, but what you could give of yourself as well. I am a great believer in the unsung heroes in so many charities and organizations, the people who make such a difference but are never recognized. I have come to believe that some of them just like it that way.

Acts of kindness like this are rare, but are a way of giving back that often makes a big difference. I often looked at ways to give back where I had a personal connection. In the nineties at St. Paul's Hospital Foundation, for example, many of the people who came to our fundraising events had a connection to the AIDS epidemic that was engulfing the city. Very few of them wore suits. Linda Dickson and I felt it was important to meet these people on the front line of the epidemic and to go deeper into what the disease was doing to our community. We often hit the road in those times to understand the extent of the devastation wreaked by AIDS on our city.

On January 25, 2021, the BC Centre for Excellence in HIV/AIDS issued a press release congratulating me on receiving the Order of Canada. In it, they mentioned how successful British Columbia has been in tackling the disease. The province once had Canada's highest rates of HIV cases, but has seen a 90 percent decrease in new cases, a 74 percent decrease in AIDS-related deaths, and a 73 percent decrease in new diagnoses.

—

ONE SUNDAY in October 2020, I happened to watch a documentary on the Humboldt accident, where a truck driver went through a rural Saskatchewan stop sign and killed sixteen members of the Humboldt Broncos high school hockey team. It was a tragic story of life lost and so much pain, and I shed a tear. And by coincidence, I recognized the mother of one of the boys who had been killed. After pondering for a while, in the late evening I reached out to Laurie Thomas by email, saying how sad I was about her loss. I was astonished to learn that she and her husband, Scott, had forgiven the driver of the truck. In their email to me, she wrote in bold font, "We believe in forgiveness."

This made me think of forgiveness as a theme in my own life. I, too, was taught to forgive, by my parents. The Humboldt story pointed out that the driver and his wife were victims of the accident, too, as he had not been properly trained to operate a vehicle of that size and power.

As a businessman and an employer, I have been disappointed by people I have hired who left my company after telling me they would stay to build a franchise. There were exceptions, like Nick Rontogiannis, an oil and gas analyst I hired straight out of the MBA program at the University of Calgary; I hired him because he was a McGill graduate first, and I was partial to McGill grads. Nick did something unusual. After being offered numerous better-paying jobs in large banks and turning them all down, he came to a point where I could not afford to keep him. So he told his prospective employer that he was going to stay with me until we found his replacement. He even took it one step further; rather than staying in downtown Vancouver when he was training with me at Salman Partners, Nick said he was going to continue living in Burnaby in a basement suite, because it was cheaper, and we were paying his rent. That's what I call a model employee.

As a Marine, I am big on loyalty; that is what "Semper fi" means. I learned a long time ago that if you cannot forgive, you cannot move forward. So, the Humboldt article and the pain my friend was suffering resonated with me. In the Marines, I gave people second chances; at the Kamehameha Schools where I taught, I gave dormitory residents second chances. My long-time assistant Anne once told me this is the quality she admires the most about me: that I "forgive and often take people back into the fold."

Over the years, I've kept all the resumés of the people who have worked for me. I am not sure why—perhaps so I could follow where they went in life. Loyalty was a big thing that I looked at when I hired them. I kept telling myself they would not stay long, and sure enough only a very few would make it to ten years with Nesbitt Thomson or Salman Partners. I spent over twenty years with both companies, but most people today move somewhere every five years on average. After getting through my initial shock of someone leaving, I would forgive and move on. In my outdoor garage at my place in Tofino, a former employee hangs up his paddleboard, which I allow him to do every time he is in Tofino. He worked for me twice, and it took me a while to forgive him when he left the first time.

Patrick Donnelly is a geologist who worked for me years ago and still calls me "Boss" every time he sees me. He and I travelled home from Cape Town together and decided to take a trip to downtown Frankfurt while we were waiting for a connection, only to miss our train stop and our flight back to Vancouver. He reminds me of that story every time I see him. Matt Sroka never worked for me, but I wish he had. Every Memorial Day and Veterans Day he calls me and thanks me for my service. He is a humble guy who was rookie of the year on the McGill football team in 2005 and once saved two people from drowning.

—

JEAN BÉLIVEAU played for one hockey team, the Montreal Canadiens, all his life, turning down opportunities to play elsewhere until he retired. Loyalty is hard to come by, and forgiveness is even rarer, but I believe you have to forgive.

My assistant Anne started to work for me when she was in her early twenties, and she has been there for me through the most difficult of times and the best. From her elevated office with a glass-encased panoramic view of Vancouver Harbour, she saw Janet, a sales person on our desk, throw a paperweight at Sam Magid; another time my previous assistant Lesley Hunter looked on as Haytham, our only black-belt employee, shut the trading desk door to fight with Sam after he said something Haytham didn't like. Anne was a gatekeeper in a high-testosterone environment, which, looking back, must have been an eye-opener for such a young woman. That trading desk at its peak was generating up to half a million dollars a month in trading commissions, enough to pay all our salaries and more. As we generated ideas there that made our clients money, we were on a roll. The legendary Wall Street fund manager John Paulson, who bet on the subprime mortgage crisis and won, was a client, as was the Caisse de dépôt, who told our head trader Bill Burk "not to assume the Caisse was not interested in our ideas" and promptly had us install a direct line to their trading desk in Montreal.

When I first read Kierkegaard's *Either/Or*, I thought he would choose one or the other, "a life filled with hedonism, such as seductive passion, and a love for music as one path, or a path of moral responsibility and a view of an exemplary life." I was surprised that he instead left the choice to the reader. My path to charity work was greatly influenced by him. When Kierkegaard spoke, kings listened.

Michael Grandin, Terry, and Jim Baillie at the Investment Dealers Association of Canada (IDA) convention, St. Andrews, NB, 2003.

Terry with Marie-José Nadeau, IDA convention, 2003.

Left to right: Ian Russell, Terry, Megan Porter, Brian Porter (Scotiabank CEO), Chris Salman, Jim Webb, and Hong Le, IDA convention, 2003.

Salman Partners' original team with Terry seated in front. Standing left to right: Bill Burk, Ian Todd, Krista MacKay, Sam Magid, and Alan Herrington, circa 2004.

Terry with Roberta Bondar, Tong Louie, and a guest, Fairmont Waterfront, Vancouver, 1997.

Terry at a corporate fundraising breakfast for St. Paul's Hospital where Ted Rogers was guest speaker, Hotel Vancouver, circa 1995.

After first long solo flight, Terry with flight instructor Helen Cernick, August 2007.

Terry with (from left to right): Chika Okereke, Robert Friedland, Lars-Eric Johansson, and Govind Friedland, in Morocco, circa 2008.

Terry and Ross Beaty at the men's hockey gold medal game between Canada and USA, 2010 Winter Olympics, in Vancouver.

ABOVE LEFT: Standing in front of painting of a Marine by Attila Richard Lukacs, 2010.

ABOVE RIGHT: With Robert Kennedy Jr. at the Swim Drink Fish charity event, Rosewood Hotel Georgia, Vancouver, 2015.

Terry with Dr. Julio Montaner, 2017.

Terry with John McCluskey, 2018.

TOP: Terry, Britannia Mine Museum, 2018. Terry was the honorary chairman of the museum's fundraising project. Britannia Mines was where Terry's father worked as a mining engineer in 1939, after graduating from McGill University.

BOTTOM: Terry receiving the Public Service Star award from Singaporean president Halimah Yacob, November 2021.

With granddaughters Amber and Esme, in front of the Terry Salman Branch of the Vancouver Public Library, 2021.

Terry with Vancouver Public Library staff: on the left, Christina de Castell, Chief Librarian, and on the right, Jenny Marsh, with the new electric cargo tricycle, 2022.

15

TIME TO MYSELF

THE WALK FROM my office in One Bentall to St. Paul's covered ten blocks and only took me twenty to thirty minutes, but I was in the fresh air, and it enabled me to come up with new ways to make the business and the foundation better. I have always been most creative when I walk or cycle to work. I would also create business or charity ideas on my forty-minute ride from West Vancouver to my downtown office. Rain or shine, I still prefer to go to work that way, crossing over the Lions Gate Bridge and often sharing its four-foot-narrow walkway with pedestrians (and sometimes other cyclists when the other lane is being repaired, a common occurrence). On very windy days I face the choice of holding on to the bridge railing or being thrown into traffic.

The rest of the ride is tame—through Stanley Park and along Beach Avenue to Hornby Street, and directly to my office—no phones, no conversations, just the sound of me shifting to a higher gear. I sometimes stop at Second Beach in Stanley Park and do a few pull-ups, although not nearly close to the number I used to do in the Marine Corps. For years I noticed a white-haired man also doing pull-ups there. Eventually I no longer saw him there, but

I continued the tradition until Covid stopped me. Bike rides are good for the soul, and the energy I felt just became stronger. Rain or cold did not stop me from enjoying the ride and the opportunity to create ideas. The silence and beauty of Stanley Park was so refreshing in the early morning.

Near Second Beach is the grave site of Indigenous poet E. Pauline Johnson. She was raised by her mother, who was of Anglican faith, so she did not attend the residential school and went on to become one of Canada's foremost poets. When she passed away, more than a hundred thousand people attended her funeral in Vancouver. I often pay tribute to her when I cycle through Stanley Park:

August is laughing across the sky,

Laughing while paddle, canoe and I,

Drift, drift

Where hills uplift

On either side of the current swift.

In the days I was going full steam on my charity work at St. Paul's and my investment banking business, it was all becoming a bit too much. One day when I was trying to work out at the gym at the Vancouver Club, a doctor friend of mine from St. Paul's noticed my discomfort and stiff movements and referred me to rheumatologist Simon Huang to be investigated for polymyalgia rheumatica (PMR). PMR is an inflammation of the joints caused by stress. I had already told Chris that something felt wrong; I couldn't reach down to lock in my telemark boots when skiing, and every time I drove to Whistler I would have to stop every ten kilometres or so to stretch my limbs. I soldiered on, but it soon became unbearable.

Dr. Huang told me that 40 percent of people who have PMR have it all their lives, while the other 60 percent recover after the first occurrence. He treated me with steroids, and slowly I started to recover, though I had gone from cycling to my office and up Cypress Mountain on the way home to doing almost nothing. By the 2005–6 ski season I somehow managed to ski thirty days, a lot less than my usual fifty, but I was on the road to recovery. In the beginning I was getting around with a walking stick, prompting Robert Friedland to comment, "I am going to take you to see my rheumatologist in Beijing."

—

I LEARNED how to ride motorcycles when I was a teenager. In fact, before I joined the Marines in 1962, I made many motorcycle trips to Plattsburgh, NY, to visit the US Marine Corps recruiter. People who ride motorcycles often are the same people who fly planes.

In my home, I keep a picture of me on my motorcycle surrounded by the staff of the hospital foundation outside St. Paul's. Linda Dickson, the executive director of the foundation at the time, has a bright face—she was trying to cheer me up as I was going through a sad withdrawal phase after leaving Nesbitt Thomson. Before Salman Partners moved to One Bentall, I had a temporary office in the hospital. I enjoyed spending time with the staff at the foundation, whom I loved, and who loved me back.

During the early nineties, when both my charitable and business work were at their peak, I unwound by riding my motorcycle. I went on rides with employees and friends. One of my favourite routes was Hope to Manning Park to Oliver. The employees who came with me tended to be more loyal, perhaps because motorcycle riders have something in common.

In 2003, I bought myself a Road King, Harley-Davidson's hundredth anniversary edition motorbike. Twelve years earlier, I had told the manager of the Harley-Davidson store that if I lived long enough, I would purchase one. As I'd hoped, the bike was a work of art. The ride was nothing like I had experienced before. The fat tire in the back and thin tire in the front gave me a stable and nimble ride. The crisp, clean feel of the gear shift is very Harley. It's an amazing ride along opening stretches.

Riding a motorcycle to Tofino in November is risky at best. When I tried it for the first time on my new Harley, I had my daughter and her husband follow me for support in an old Land Rover. I was very happy to see them and to get some blood circulation back into my fingers, as there was frost on both sides of the road.

—

I'VE ALWAYS been fascinated with surfing. I bought my first board at a surf shop at Cannon Beach in Oregon, on a cycling trip along the iconic US Route 101 with a group of people celebrating their fortieth birthdays. I was in my fifties then, but I managed to beat everyone riding my vintage professional Raleigh road bike. I was so far ahead that I had time to stop and buy a classic longboard signed by Donald Takayama, a pro surfer and legendary surfboard shaper. The guides of the cycling tour company Backroads were able to suspend my board in the support van.

I had always wanted to buy a house on a surfing beach. In the nineties, when I finally had enough money to fulfill this dream, Chris and I travelled the world to find our ideal beach-front property. After visiting the little town called Hanalei along Nā Pali Coast of the Hawaiian Island of Kauai, we decided to look at beaches north of Sydney in Australia. We visited Surfers Paradise, just south of Brisbane, on our way to Noosa, and even went as far as

Port Douglas, another 1,800 kilometres north. But Chris thought these spots were all too far away. She was right; my life as an investment banker did not allow me to pick a place too far from home.

We settled instead on the west coast of Vancouver Island, a magical surf spot. I have always loved end-of-the-road towns, and Tofino was one I could not forget. Back in 1987, when Tasha and Krista were in their early teens, we went camping in Pacific Rim National Park just south of Tofino. Not too long after that, I bought a cabin nearby for $275,000, on Chesterman Beach, where people surf literally right outside my window. Linda, my realtor at the time, said I would have to bid full price to get it because there was another offer. Chris still thought it was too far away from home, but I bought it anyway.

I eventually built a new place in Tofino that enabled me to make some of the best decisions of my life, surrounded by the peace and serenity of the place, the sound of waves, and the fog-horn miles away offshore on the Lennard Island lighthouse. It was one of the first places where I started to think about charity work. Despite my monetary success at that time, something was missing.

I love the people I've got to know in Tofino. Jake Bower, one of many Vietnam draft dodgers, ended up there because he likes to surf, and Tofino was one of the few Canadian places he heard had good waves. I liked Jake, but most of the time he took me fishing instead of surfing. Allister Fernie, who owns the Storm Surf shop in Tofino, repaired my Takayama longboard once after it was discoloured by a lamp.

I first met Charlie Mickey of the Hesquiaht Band after he had carved a totem pole that was raised at the edge of Pacific Rim National Park. The totem is not there anymore but a friend told me Charlie had a similar one at his house in Port Alberni and suggested I go talk to him. When I saw his totem pole, it reminded me so much of the one at the park entrance, I bought it and took it home. I noted that Charlie had not signed the pole, so a few years later, he came back with his wife, Caroline, for tea and cookies to celebrate the signing.

The last time I saw Bruce Ramsay, my old friend from our Calgary days, was when he visited us in Tofino. We had dinner at the Wickaninnish Inn, a hotel on a spectacular rocky outcrop at the north end of Chesterman Beach that I was originally opposed to being built. With a few of my neighbours on Lynn Road, I fought the construction plans in the 1990s, thinking the development would spoil the natural beauty of the beach. The vote was a tie, which the mayor broke by voting for the hotel. He was a fisherman, and when I called him before the vote asking him not to support the application, he told me we needed the business so he was for it. The next day I called him, and he told me, "They sunk my boat in the harbour." I told him he should have voted against it. To this day, the RCMP have not found out who sunk his boat. All these years later, the Wickaninnish is my neighbour, and I am proud to have it there and take people like Bruce there for dinner to admire the stunning views. Chris agrees—though she never signed the petition against building it.

Sometimes on a clear day, I fly from Tofino airport to Nootka Sound and back, to look at Yuquot, also known as Friendly Cove. Once, I saw an amazing pod of whales there. Yuquot was the summer home of the Ahousaht, who speak the Nuu-chah-nulth language. The word Ahousaht means "facing opposite from the ocean" or "people living with their backs to the land and mountains," according to the Canadian Encyclopedia online. In 1778, Chief Maquinna of the Nuu-chah-nulth met Captain Cook at Yuquot and established a friendly trading route.

The West Coast clears my mind of stress and opens new visions and ideas. It is a magical place.

16

FUELLED BY COMMITMENT

THE SALMAN PARTNERS legacy in mining started in 1994 and continued through the 2000s. We hired another analyst by the name of Ray Goldie, who expanded our publications to the *Morning Metal Notes*, which had an audience of around five thousand mining executives around the world. It was one of the liveliest publications the firm ever produced.

Rodney Stevens was selling cell phones when he cold called me. He had completed the required academic portions of a CFA and was looking for a place to gain work experience so he could use his CFA designation. I hired him as an analyst, without yet knowing what he should analyze. One sunny afternoon after the market closed, Rodney, another female analyst, and I decided to go for a run in a place called Rabbit Lane, in a park leading to the Capilano Dam in North Vancouver. The purpose of the run was to discuss with Rodney what he was going to cover. He said he was thinking of Newmont. I told him, "You will be the thirtieth analyst covering that company, and no one will care. Silver is trading at seven dollars, and I think it will go higher, you should cover emerging silver companies. We can get paid for that, whereas we will never get paid covering Newmont."

On November 11, 2005, we published a fifty-eight-page silver company report based on Rodney's work as analyst. The report became one of the best calls our company ever made—as a result, two silver companies were sold, one went bankrupt, and the others became multimillion-ounce producers. One in the last group was Silvercorp, which today has a market cap of $2.5 billion. Rui Feng, the CEO, had called me and asked me to send an analyst to China to look at their operations. He told me to have an open mind, and shortly thereafter, Rodney was on a plane to Beijing. There were many other silver companies we covered, analyzed by Haytham Hodaly.

Research was my first love in the investment industry. From Nesbitt Thomson's research department in the seventies to the day we gave up our brokerage in 2016, I remained as director or co-director of research. I became a mentor to many research analysts, bankers, and salesmen. In the early nineties, Salman Partners became an early sponsor to many junior mining companies, many of which grew from mid-tier to large cap companies: Alamos Gold, Pan American Silver, Nevsun, and First Quantum, to name a few. From an investment banking perspective, we focused on following exploration companies that were actually finding the resources because the major companies were spending less and less on exploration in the nineties.

In 1997, we lost half of our capital on a company we researched called Newport Petroleum, a story I told earlier. Calgary was a competitive place in those days as the charter banks had purchased a number of independent dealers, and regional dealers like Peters & Co. and Salman Partners had to be incredibly competitive. One major firm competing for a piece of business with me sent a call girl to the CEO's hotel room, hoping to win his favour and gain the underwriting position. The bank letters were our saving grace, but they did not stay around much longer. Looking back, I had the good fortune to recover from the Newport fiasco and go on to create a very respectable investment firm.

In 1997 I was asked to join the board of Southam Inc., a newspaper company that owned the *Vancouver Sun*, the Vancouver *Province*, the *Montreal Gazette*, and other notable Canadian dailies. The company was owned in part by Hollinger Inc., led by Conrad Black and David Radler, one of the original shareholders of Salman Partners and the reason I got involved with the Southam board. We led a major $200 million income trust transaction with our partners at CIBC. The deal sold out quickly and became one of the largest private placements we ever did. I learned a lot about the newspaper business in those days as I was on the Southam board when they created a new Canadian daily, the *National Post*. I have a framed copy of the front page of the first issue, featuring astronaut John Glenn. Hollinger, the parent company of Southam, had its elegant head office in Toronto, complete with an Andy Warhol painting of a young Conrad. Joining me as new members to an already prestigious board in 1997 were Richard Rohmer, Ron Southern, and Harry Steele; this was a board that truly represented the Canadian establishment from coast to coast. The annual meeting of Southam was an elegant affair, and in those days Conrad Black was at the top of his game. When asked by a reporter if he had a business card, he replied that he didn't—"Everyone knows who I am." He was right. Several years later, when Hollinger bought out the minority of Southam, I left the board.

—

AS ONE of my Marines three times wounded stepped up to receive his third Purple Heart from his commanding officer, the officer asked, "How did you hurt yourself, Marine?"

"Playing baseball, sir," was his answer.

I learned how to play baseball in Vietnam. We played as a platoon and all followed the lead of my radio operator, who was a fastball pitcher on one of the Baltimore Orioles major league farm team. So, on our rare afternoons off, in the middle of a bloody war zone far from home, we learned how to catch and throw and bat and run bases.

These young Americans were some of the best players. The thing about baseball is, no matter your walk in life, you are equal on the field. So, when I started in the investment business, I always had a softball team. Whether a senior investment banker or working in the back office, all were equal. It enabled me to reach those with whom I otherwise would not have had the chance to communicate. It is often said that you can learn more about your organization when you reach the lowest level of employees and work your way back up. Softball allowed me to do that.

—

ROSS BEATY was a strong supporter of western-based brokerage firms. So, one day in 1999, he called me and told me that he'd like to raise some money and asked if we were interested. I said yes, but I had a problem—I was about to hike the West Coast Trail in Pacific Rim National Park, so could he wait five days? After a long pause, he agreed.

I discussed my first hike on the WCT earlier. This time, I thought about who to contact as I climbed up the ladder system, and I lined up expressions of interest while I was resting on the beach. Although cellphone reception was almost non-existent, I managed to get through to a few potential investors, much to the dismay of my fellow hikers. I was putting it all together in my head as I had a shower in a waterfall, in the one place on the trail where you can do this, with the surf from the ocean right in front of your eyes. Ross, who is an environmentalist, allowed me to do this while he was waiting for my return to complete the transaction. A week later, we launched the first cross-border Pan American Silver deal.

The company's market cap went from very little to a whopping $6.8 billion today. And it was not just Pan American—all of Ross's companies have been acquired, creating billions of dollars of value for investors. His latest one is Equinox Gold, with a market cap of $2.54 billion. One of the most important aspects in mining is to bet on the right horse, and I've had the fortune to bet on a number of good horses, with Ross Beaty way up there at the top.

Ross became one of my closest friends, not only because of business, but because we have so much in common. My association with him has spanned more than thirty years, and in many ways he is an inspiration. We are kindred spirits who love hockey, skiing, and the great outdoors. We both are philanthropists and give back in different ways, and the only thing we disagree on is the existence of God. Salman Partners followed and participated in almost all of his companies, including Global Copper Corp and Northern Peru Copper. To me, Ross is a mentor and a role model first and foremost. He has spent his life giving to many causes that focus on our environment, creating more green spaces, and making our world a better place. He also supports a number of universities, notably making a major donation to UBC, where a number of buildings are named after him and his family, including the Beaty Biodiversity Museum.

Ross is totally committed to growing his Sitka Foundation, named after the large Sitka spruce trees that grow on the west coast of Vancouver Island (poetically, I saw many of them while hiking the West Coast Trail). If you are ever in one of those forests, you feel like you are in a cathedral. The Sitka Foundation has given over $5 million to seventy-four different Canadian environmental groups.

Unlike me and many others, Ross shuns expensive toys. He had a Porsche Boxster once, but he and his wife gave it up because it was not good for the environment. She switched to a Nissan Leaf. A number of years ago, he rode a motorcycle along the Silk Road from China to Europe, a 6,500-kilometre ride that took him several months. I went to his welcome home party on his return. Recently, Ross gave up his position as the chair of Pan American Silver, the company he founded so many years ago. On the chairlift not too long ago, he told me he was going to focus more on Equinox and his charitable work. It sounded like he was freeing himself from all his previous commitments.

Ross Beaty has achieved so much and yet never brags about it. A few years ago, I had the pleasure to go to Toronto to see him inducted in the Canadian Mining Hall of Fame. It was hosted by another mining legend, Pierre Lassonde. In introducing Ross, Pierre couldn't help but point out how frugal he was compared to all other inductees he was going to introduce that night. We often go to hockey games together. We circle the block a few times looking for a cheap parking spot because we don't want to pay the exorbitant thirty-dollar fee charged just outside the stadium.

On December 23, 2018, a windstorm struck my house in West Vancouver, pushing the ocean water over my yard break and into the basement. My library of more than a thousand books was destroyed, including books from Captain James Cook's three great voyages and the original book of my Marines Corps graduating class from Parris Island. Various precious paintings were also ruined—ironically including one by a Shanghai artist depicting a dragon calming the sea.

In one stroke, climate change became a reality for me, and I wanted to educate myself on how I could help. Ross sent me an email of encouragement suggesting ways I could get involved: "support nature and mitigate climate change potential and global warming." He went on to recommend a few things I could do, including donating to NGOs and environmental groups that are doing good things, like his own Sitka Foundation. Another way to give time is to serve on their boards; Ross supports both the Pacific Salmon Foundation and the BC Parks Foundation, which he currently chairs. "Finally, you can invest in good companies that are doing good things," Ross told me. "And some of them are quite profitable."

So, looking forward, I am eyeing opportunities in the conservation and climate change fields, even though so far I've done absolutely nothing except buy my wife an electric car for her seventieth birthday. I hope to add proposals to my Essential Needs Foundation in due course. Whether you believe in climate change or not, rapid population growth alone has taxed and will continue impacting our environment like never before.

I love the sound of rain falling on a copper roof. It doesn't have the same sound on any other metal. Copper absorbs the noise and sounds slightly muffled, almost like it welcomes the rain. It is so easy to sleep with that sound. I live in a rainforest, and I wonder if climate change will change it all. I never took climate change seriously, more out of lack of knowledge. But in helping to make the world a better place and do the right thing, I now believe climate change causes have to be a priority.

—

ON MY desk is an engraved silver Tiffany paperweight that was a gift to celebrate the closing of two financings for a company called Nevsun Resources in 2002. In my house is a painting by the Indigenous artist Roy Henry Vickers, one of two that Craig Angus of Nevsun gave me to celebrate the closing. Called *Watchman*, it shows an eagle looking over the waters at the snow-capped mountains on the west coast of Vancouver Island. Like many of our original financings, Nevsun became a large company. In 2002, we went to West Africa to tour their operations in Ghana and Mali. This was one of the most enjoyable mining trips I've ever been on. With the help of a rented plane from the Ashanti Goldfields Corporation, we toured Nevsun's operations in both countries. We enjoyed time with the miners in Ghana, our first stop, and had dinner one night with people from Ashanti. The next day we were due to head to Mali.

In the middle of the night, I was surprised to hear someone knocking on my door. Through the peephole, I saw an attractive Black woman. She asked if I would like some company and did not want to take no for an answer. I refused to let her in, and, finally, an hour later, she left.

The next day, we boarded the plane to Mali. The hotel we stayed at in Bamako, the Radisson Blu, was bombed in 2015 by Islamists. After we toured the mines, we spent another night, paid our exit tax, and left for Accra in Ghana.

I experienced one of the worst storms in my life on that flight, including a call from the Bamako immigration officers asking us to come back to pay additional taxes. We voted on whether to return to Mali or continue to Accra. We continued onward because we figured that Mali had a very limited air force, even though the president was a pilot himself. Nevsun became a multibillion-dollar company and was eventually taken over by Zijin in 2018 for $1.8 billion.

17

A NAME FOR ALL SEASONS

THE CHAIRS OF the Investment Dealers Association of Canada (IDA) have been pillars of the Canadian financial establishments for over a hundred years. They included Brian Aune and Brian Steck, my friends and mentors from Nesbitt Thomson. As the CEO of a small Vancouver-based firm, I was surprised and humbled in 2002 to be asked to be the new vice chair, knowing the profound history of this organization.

The man who asked me to take on the role, Jacques Ménard, was then the CEO of BMO Quebec. The first time I met him, I was so impressed with how he conducted his role as the chair of IDA. He had a manner and presence that was above those of most investment bankers. He was truly a gentleman and had honorary degrees from six universities as well as the Order of Canada at the companion level.

I was sad to see Jacques leave his position as chair of IDA but honoured to have him appoint me as the new chair during a visit to my place in Whistler in 2002. During those few days we spent together, my wife and I got to know him and his wife, Marie-José, well. Jacques was one of these people in my life that I really wished I had spent more time with but never could because of our busy schedules.

The investiture ceremony was held at the Manoir Richelieu in La Malbaie, Quebec, and conducted by Jacques Ménard. He had explained to me, "The IDA of Canada is a self-regulatory body and representative of the securities industry. The association's role is to foster fair, efficient, and competitive capital markets by encouraging participation in the savings and investment process and by ensuring the integrity of the marketplace." It has since split into two organizations: the Investment Industry Regulatory Organization of Canada (IIROC) and the Investment Industry Association of Canada (IIAC).

First built in 1899 and then burned down in 1928, Hôtel Fairmont Le Manoir Richelieu was rebuilt a year later, during the Great Depression, to a design by the famous architect John Smith Archibald. Some hundred and fifty kilometres north of Quebec City, the hotel sits on a cliff overlooking the St. Lawrence River in the Charlevoix region, known for its beautiful landscapes, arts and crafts, and fine cheeses. Although Jacques and I had both worked for BMO, we had never worked together; he came from the Burns Fry side, and I came from the Nesbitt Thomson side. But we became friends during the time we worked at IDA. He was the most elegant and plugged-in investment banker I've ever met.

The IDA was originally a trade association supporting broker dealers that eventually became a self-regulatory body. I spent three years working there while Jacques was the chairman. I learned a lot from him about the industry. I had come a long way from my first IDA convention in Jasper in the 1980s, when I was just a participant filling in for someone who did not show up. In 2002, my role with the IDA was much more intense. At the time, it was a dynamic organization, and I wanted to get the message out that we had a serious role to play in the capital markets and should continue to be a trade association and a self-regulatory organization (SRO). There was pressure on the industry, and I wanted to put the IDA in the strongest possible light. During that year, I gave six speeches, including a major one at Canadian Club Toronto.

We had a tough board meeting in Montreal where the chair of the Ontario Securities Commission, David Brown, read us the riot act, telling us that we would have to get our acts together as a self-regulating body. Jacques took that meeting seriously and added strong members to the IDA board, including a senior officer of Quebec Hydro. Jacques understood the responsibility in being the chair of this organization and made his mark spearheading the organization to a stronger role in enforcement.

The IDA board of directors at the time included some prominent Canadians: Brian Porter, today the CEO of Scotiabank; Marie-José Nadeau, member of the Order of Canada, and later a member of the World Energy Council; and Joe Oliver, the minister of finance of Canada after Jim Flaherty. So, I felt Canada was well served by the IDA and would have preferred the organization to stay intact, but then I'm a Marine and love long-standing organizations with so much history. The IDA lapel pin and the gavel and cufflinks I received when I became IDA chair are reminders of that proud history.

The job at the IDA was the most intense travel commitment I had in my entire career. From May to October 2002, Jacques and I travelled Canada from coast to coast, as well as to the US and the UK to talk to regulators and financial practitioners in those markets. Jacques handled these trips and meetings effortlessly. He generally was interested in the subject. He got along with Joe Oliver, the IDA president, and Ian Russell, the senior VP. Fluent in English and French, Jacques was a master of bringing together people from across the spectrum of the political arena without offending anyone.

Perhaps Jacques's greatest legacy was his charitable work, which inspired me. The *Montreal Gazette* put it so well: "Best known for his four-decade career as a banker and investment dealer, Ménard carved out a parallel path of extraordinary breadth that spanned philanthropy, community involvement, education, health care and the arts." While I was active in charity work long before I met him, his actions helped me go forward with the charity work I was doing. We talked about giving back and shared the same passion, but in different areas.

During the year in which I was chair, I was on the road constantly, telling the story of IDA to investors, regulators, corporations, and politicians. It was an amazing time of my life. One day, I flew from Vancouver to Saint John to give a speech to the Chamber of Commerce the following morning. After this long journey with a cold, I arrived in the New Brunswick town in the evening with no dinner. I knocked on the door of a restaurant that was closed. In typical Maritime fashion, they were having a private cod dinner and invited me in to share it. I had an engaging breakfast presentation with the members of the chamber of commerce and headed on to Halifax, Nova Scotia, for a board meeting and a tour of Pier 21, a magnificent reconstruction of the original immigration point of entry to Canada from Europe.

Pier 21 was chaired by Ruth Goldbloom, who was on the IDA board. She had made the museum bloom with history. Ruth almost single-handedly turned this rundown waterfront facility into a national museum, including reconstructions of trains going from Halifax across Canada full of immigrants telling their individual stories. It was so impressive to see what she had done. You got a real sense of the trauma they must have experienced as new arrivals and how much they really helped to build this country. To go from Europe to Halifax and on to the Prairies must have been so overwhelming. The audio stories made you feel like you were there with them.

Over the winter, I flew to Saskatoon and gave a speech to the chamber of commerce. There, I made the argument for regulators and the government to reduce costs—such as business taxes and insurance, as well as those related to employee benefits—to small businesses. It was such a clear day, and I could not believe how beautiful it was at twenty below zero. I took a walk down the main street and visited the University of Saskatchewan to get an update on the research that they were doing. This was Canada's heartland, a place I hadn't visited since I took the train cross-country in 1979. I brought up the same case at the Rotary Club of Vancouver, and I also presented a case on how Vancouver could attract more head offices.

Because the IDA was both a trade association and a regulator, it had a lot of clout. The big event in the calendar was the annual IDA conference, which was an opportunity to get together on a national stage with our colleagues, regulators, and other industry participants. It was one of the few times that you could get together with the head of various securities commissions. All my speeches came to a head in the one I gave defending the IDA's self-regulatory role at the 2003 IDA conference, held in June at St. Andrews by-the-Sea in New Brunswick, a beautiful place that was the home of Alexander Graham Bell, the inventor of the telephone and founder of the Bell telephone company. Also nearby was the summer home of Franklin Roosevelt, situated on Campobello Island in the Bay of Fundy.

Thanks to Ian Russell, our senior VP, we were able to put together a group of speakers never seen in the history of the IDA, and the IDA board let me run with it. The keynote was given by Jim Webb, a Marine Corps officer and war hero who was awarded the Navy Cross, a Silver Star, two Bronze Stars, and two Purple Hearts for his actions in Vietnam. I have a picture of him and me in my office, which he signed "Semper Fi, Terry." He was secretary of the Navy under Ronald Reagan and told the audience that the war the Americans had started with Iraq was going to ignite a thousand-year-long conflict with the Arab world. Also at that convention was the president of Cantor Fitzgerald, a powerful Wall Street brokerage at the time, who was late because he had travelled to St. John's, Newfoundland, instead of Saint John, New Brunswick. We enjoyed his talk very much, especially the portion about the 1,800-kilometre detour he took by mistake.

—

FOR ME, the IDA was a five-year journey that allowed me to give back to an industry that has given me so much financial freedom, and most importantly the opportunity to further the charities I cared about. I always felt more comfortable trying to make the SRO better. I wanted to get away from those clichéd images of the industry: middle-aged, white-haired male brokers ripping off a young couple who had just opened a brokerage account—easy targets as they often made uninformed investment decisions.

Things were about to get worse as I found myself being sued by retail investor advocates—along with our vice chair, Kim Anthony, and Joe Oliver, the president of the IDA. Fortunately for us, an Ontario court threw out the action, stating that a regulatory body could not be sued.

My commitment to IDA had a bigger purpose: I was trying to promote the role of small businesses in Canada. Small businesses are and continue to be the engine of our economy, creating more jobs than any other sector. In addition, many innovations in the capital markets are produced as a result of the regulatory competition created by the different securities commissions across the country and the IDA. It was Monty Gordon of Gordon Capital, for instance, who created the bought deal, which is still the preferred underwriting option by issuers. And the securities commissions in Alberta and British Columbia were the ones to first pioneer the private placement, four-month-hold instrument that eliminated the need for prospectuses. Today, most financings done in Canada are done in this manner, especially with the smaller companies. Many of my IDA colleagues supported this initiative.

As my one-year term as chair was coming to an end, I was grateful to pass the torch to Kim Anthony. I had enjoyed my role on the national stage very much, especially because it gave me the opportunity to build lasting friendships. On my desk is a large photo album of some of the many people I got to know during my term. In June 2003, when my responsibilities as IDA chair ended, I received two letters that made me feel as if I had fulfilled my role with honour. The first came from Jim Baillie, an outside director of the IDA, who wrote, "You put enormous energy into the job. Perhaps more importantly, you worked in a thoughtful way, with great sensitivities (both individual and political). It was truly a magnificent performance." The second letter came from Tom Atkinson, the CEO of Market Regulation Services, who wrote, "I want to congratulate you on the great job you did while serving as Chair of the IDA board. You made a real difference." He went on, "As regulators we rarely hear that we are doing a good job so I thought I would take this opportunity. At the IDA Annual Meeting, a number of people were talking about the considerable energy and enthusiasm you brought to this important position." I went back to work at Salman Partners and on my giving-back initiatives. I continued working in a minor way for IDA as I stayed on the board as the past chair for another year.

The view from my office on the twenty-first floor of the HSBC Canada Building in downtown Vancouver was hard to forget. We even had an outside balcony to savour the outlook of the Lions mountain peaks above North Vancouver and the harbour below. From the beautiful village of St. Andrews by-the-Sea to Vancouver, I took in Canada from coast to coast—what a journey!

—

IN 2003, Salman Partners participated in twenty-seven transactions that raised $1.2 billion for companies, a number of which were lead managers. By the end of the year, after paying out millions of dollars in bonuses, the company's capital had grown to $13 million, from $1 million in 1995. Business continued to grow steadily. We were a small player but continued to be a major actor in the mining sector. The IDA enhanced our presence and enabled me to have a vision on the national scale. It's hard to not think about the IDA as a giving back commitment to the industry that served me so well.

In the summer of 2019, Chris and I had planned to go to her nephew's wedding in Pictou, Nova Scotia. I called Jacques Ménard and asked him if we could get together on our way back home if we stopped in Montreal. He liked the idea and suggested we spend a few days enjoying the fall colours in the Laurentian Mountains south of Montreal, where he had a place. In August, I called him back to discuss us getting together, but he said, "There's been a change of plans, I am first in line for a lung transplant." Needless to say, I was very shocked. Before I could say anything, he said he would take prayers from any denomination. I told him I was Anglican, not unlike his Catholic faith, and would certainly pray for him. Meanwhile, I told him, my wife's nephew had found out a few days earlier that he had testicular cancer, but he was going forward with the wedding anyway.

After Jacques received his lung transplant, I was told by his assistant in Montreal that he was recovering well in the hospital. She later told me that despite recovering for a while, he unfortunately had a relapse and died shortly afterwards. I'd told him at one point, "I'm trying to spend as much time with people like you as possible." Sadly, I never saw Jacques Ménard again. I think about him often.

18

THE UNTHINKABLE

Learning to Fly

IT'S BEEN SAID that once you get a taste for flight, you'll forever cast your eyes skyward with a longing to return. It's a sentiment often attributed to Leonardo da Vinci, and one with which I whole heartedly agree. On August 18, 2008, I officially met all the requirements to get a Class 3 pilot's licence. I had just completed the long solo flight over Washington, from Wenatchee to Yakima and back, a distance of 181 miles, assuming you take a straight line and there is no turbulence or deviation, which is most unlikely in the Columbia Valley. My flight time was a little more than two hours. Two years after I started learning to fly in Squamish, I was a pilot.

In my house at Whistler is a framed shirt, one that was literally taken off my back when I completed my long solo flight. My instructor, Helen, had an artist paint the graphics, which show my plane, the date, and the call sign, CGTKS (the last three letters being my initials). A few hours earlier, she had radioed me to tell me to go around and try it again as the landing approach was not to her liking. No wonder she was perspiring and sounding nervous when I finally landed. Helen taught me how to soar and fly with confidence.

Sometimes when I fly, I think of my mother and I say a prayer for her. She was the pillar of my Anglican faith. My fear of flying started in Vietnam and continued many years after I left combat in Chu Lai in January 1966. When I joined Nesbitt Thomson in 1973, I avoided planes and took the train everywhere. My first commercial flight after returning from Vietnam was from Montreal to Boston in 1974. My time in the Hueys was always on my mind.

The open doors of the chopper had never bothered me. But just being up there going from place to place while the Viet Cong shot the occasional tracer rounds up at us, though they were almost always out of range, was stressful. In Vietnam, helicopters were the army's lifeblood, the way we travelled in the combat zone. The sound of one lifting off a carrier in the sunlight gave me a feeling of power, and yet it was a feeling of vulnerability as well. The choppers brought our food and mail in, and our dead and wounded out. We heard stories about South Vietnamese army helicopters taking Viet Cong sympathizers up in the air to try to get information from them; sometimes they would push them out of the helicopters because they didn't like what they heard. Often the helicopter pilots helped us out in difficult situations. The helicopters were incredibly important for my 81mm mortar unit because mortars are heavy and moving around with them on the ground in the extreme jungle heat was treacherous.

Nobel laureate John Steinbeck wrote about the pilots in his dispatches from Vietnam for *Newsday*, that he was envious of the way they maneuvered their planes, weaving and turning like birds, in complete control, and with a coordination as delicate and hands as deft as musicians. He wrote of how much he wished to have such skills—he reported they made him jealous—and how much he wished to fly as well.

Well, the last thing I ever wanted to do was to fly, let alone a helicopter. The skill of the Marine Corps helicopter pilot is beyond dispute, but I never took Steinbeck's view; I saw way too many accidents, with Hueys being shot down or malfunctioning under different conditions. More and more, I would rather have been on the ground, and yet every time there was a lift-off, I was grateful we were moving away from a dangerous place to safer ground, and I couldn't help but feel the power and grace of the helicopter taking flight, before my fear of flying set in.

I ultimately became a pilot to bury the demons of the Vietnam War. My experience is best described in the letter I wrote to the president of Cirrus Aircraft, the manufacturer of my airplane, in which I described "this incredible journey that started all those years ago on a makeshift tarmac in a Vietnamese jungle." I really meant it when I ended by writing, "I shall never forget the caring people who made it happen."

I enjoy flying as there is nothing like it. British Columbia is a magical place to fly, with the sea and the majestic rivers and their deep valleys to navigate between snow-capped mountain ranges so wild and pristine it seems no one has been there before. Flying is almost spiritual, giving me a peace of mind far away from the troubles of life. With just a tip of the wing, you can see a new spectacular view that was not available a minute ago. I've always told people that flying is the perfect Covid activity as you are a long way away from the virus, perfectly by yourself.

This poem I think of often:

HIGH FLIGHT

Oh! I have slipped the surly bonds of earth
And danced the skies on laughter-silvered wings;
Sunward I've climbed, and joined the tumbling mirth
Of sun-split clouds—and done a hundred things
You have not dreamed of—wheeled and soared and swung
High in the sunlit silence. Hov'ring there
I've chased the shouting wind along, and flung
My eager craft through footless halls of air.

Up, up the long delirious, burning blue,
I've topped the windswept heights with easy grace
Where never lark, or even eagle flew—
And, while with silent lifting mind I've trod
The high unsurpassed sanctity of space,
Put out my hand and touched the face of God.

Pilot Officer John Gillespie Magee

Magee was a Yale student whose parents were Quaker mission-aries in China. He decided to join the Royal Canadian Air Force to fight the Nazis. After one of his flights, he wrote this poem and sent it to his mother. It is the official poem of the RCAF and the RAF today.

I've had the good fortune of having two female flight instruct-ors, Collette Morin and Helen Cernick. Why they wanted to teach me how to fly, I will never know. Collette, my first instructor, taught me how to fly out of her hometown of Squamish, which means "big wind" in the Indigenous language of the Salish people of southwestern BC. The tiny runway sits at the end of Howe Sound surrounded by water and mountains. No wonder Collette told me, "If you can learn how to fly in Squamish, you can fly any-where." Over Howe Sound, she taught to me to stall the Cessna 172 and turn it upside down to simulate a spin. The first time, I told her, "I can't do this anymore." She quickly shot back, "You can do this—you're a Marine."

I made the mistake of buying a plane before I had a licence. I bought a Cirrus SR20 when the Canadian dollar was par with the US dollar. Collette flew the plane back from Duluth, Minnesota, and we continued our training. I then began lessons with Helen and moved the plane to Bellingham in the State of Washington to obtain more Cirrus training.

Flying did not come easily to me, but I finally learned to do it in the Columbia Valley, where the deep valleys and the ocean create a lot of turbulence. I always asked Helen why we had to go through the valley. She was trying to teach me how to get out of a valley when you are boxed in by mountains, a terrifying situation if you are too low and can't turn around. As I came in for landing in Wenatchee on my first solo, I could hear Helen on the radio instructing me to ensure I made the proper landing, her breath sounding strained and nervous.

The first time you fly solo in the US, the practice is to tear the shirt off your back. But Helen took the shirt off my back, and had an artist paint a picture of me and my plane landing in Wenatchee. It took over four decades, but I had finally managed to bury the demons from the Vietnam War.

In 2010, I flew a Cirrus SR22, much like my SR20, around the Hawaiian Island of Kauai and over Niʻihau, an island owned by the Robinson family that is reserved for native Hawaiians only. As someone who spent many years training in and exploring Hawaii, it was a real thrill to fly over Niʻihau, the only island I have never been able to visit. There is no running water on the island, and Hawaiians live there in the ancient, traditional way. There is no cellphone or radio service, though as I looked down, I saw a couple of pickup trucks. I felt grateful to have had that opportunity. I made a turn over Niʻihau, and as I ascended the deep valleys of Kauai on a beautiful rare sunny day, I was able to see the wettest place on Earth, Mount Waialeale, which receives around 460 inches of rain every year.

A few months ago, as I flew over Long Beach in Pacific Rim National Park just south of my house in Tofino, I couldn't help but think of Ruth Glenen, Brian Aune's wife and my old friend. The last time I saw her in Tofino was for my daughter Krista's wedding. She had told me she wanted to drive Brian out to visit us here when she was well enough, but unfortunately she was never able to do it. As I watched the surfers below from the air, I was reminded of the ritual called the Paddle-Out, adopted from an ancient Hawaiian tradition. In it, surfers form a circle in the ocean to celebrate the life of someone very much loved who has died. I recalled reading the chain of emails I received after Ruth passed away, which made me feel everyone's love for her, just like the circle in the surfers' celebration of life.

I first met Ruth in 1973, when I was still a grad student at the University of Hartford. She was pivotal in my life from then on. Without her, I would have never met Brian Aune, who became one of the most important people in my life, and my closest friend. Ruth organized my first encounters with him in the early days and always made sure that he had time for me. When I started to work at Nesbitt Thomson in 1973, Ruth continued to aid me in numerous ways, including helping with my daughters, who were toddlers at the time. She continued to support us her entire life, even when my daughters became university students in Montreal years later.

Ruth was a pillar of strength with incredible organizational skills. She was always there for me and was foundational to my career. Both Brian and Ruth were my life-long friends. Whenever I received an award or achieved something notable in my life, they were always there celebrating with me. When I auctioned off my Breitling Navitimer watch, which I used to solo my first flight as a pilot, to the Vancouver Public Library Foundation, unbeknown to me at the time, Brian and Ruth bid on the watch—they gifted it to me at Christmas that same year. I am grateful to their son, Jonathan, and the Aune Foundation for this incredible gift in Ruth's name to support female entrepreneurs.

—

ONE OF the challenges I faced in becoming a pilot was taking off and landing in Tofino. I had bought my place there long before, but it was only in learning to fly that I realized how deadly fog can be, and how quickly it can come and go. I had often wondered why the Tofino airport has three runways; it turns out it is in an old air force base built during World War II, and the three runways gave pilots options for landing if the others were fogged in. I was told that many of the pilots trained for WWII came from the prairies and had never seen mountains of fog, so many lost their lives near Tofino.

One bright sunny day, Chris, my flight instructor Helen, and I decided to fly to Victoria from Tofino for lunch. By the time we came back, all three runways were covered in fog. Helen, with the most experience, took over from me to try to land. She asked Chris and me if we could see the runway, but we couldn't see a thing from three hundred feet. So we had to land in nearby Port Alberni.

Another obstacle to flying is smoke, which has increased exponentially in British Columbia recently due to extreme forest fires. A couple of summers ago as I took off from Kelowna's airport, I was shocked to see that the smoke all around me was so thick and dark that I could not make out the mountains I would have to climb over. The forecast was supposed to be VFR (visual flight rules), but my eyes were telling me something else. I asked the Kelowna tower if I could continue to climb over Okanagan Lake to get enough clearance to cross the mountains, which I still could not even see. After receiving the green light, I rose to 9,500 feet, just above the smoke, and headed towards Vancouver. All I could think was how will I find a hole in the smoke to get down once I reach Vancouver airspace, as the smoke from the forest fires had quickly moved westward.

As I flew out of Tofino's airport in mid-September last year, I could not help but reflect on how beautiful the view of the coast is and how often the colours change. The view is never the same.

Sometimes the ocean is silver-blue, and other times dark grey. More often than not, the fog is nearby, making its way to shore. I could see the place on Chesterman Beach where western sandpipers had assembled en masse a few weeks earlier, as they have done for eternity. My son-in-law Angus, who is a bit of a bird expert, tells me they stop here on their way from the Aleutian Islands, Alaska, en route to Mexico. They also stop at Boundary Bay, site of the airport where I land after I leave Tofino. As I informed air traffic control that I was going to climb to 7,500 feet, these little birds were taking the same route. Angus told me that the young ones come a few weeks later. You cannot help but marvel at nature when you see these tiny birds, each one only a couple inches long, making their way on the same path as an aviator.

—

AS A pilot, every time you receive a letter from Transport Canada, you take a deep breath and hope for the best. One of my friends, a Green Beret Vietnam veteran and a senior Federal Aviation Administration (FAA) doctor, once told me that the FAA did not want you flying. As every pilot knows, as you get older, the requirements for your medical approvals become more stringent. Regional Aviation Medical Officer Dr. Rani Tolton sent me a letter asking for a number of clarifications on my medical history after my aviation medical doctor, Dr. John Corey, had signed off on my approval.

Dr. Corey had given me a whisper test, which most pilots do not take seriously as it is a basic hearing test. To offset the impact of some minor hearing loss, I decided to fit myself for hearing aids and contacted a hearing specialist, although noise cancellation headsets have a similar effect. In her very pleasant letter, Dr. Tolton told me that I could not fly until she received more information—new blood, hearing, and eye test results, and a report from my audiologist.

Flying has always been a challenge for me, and the little hearing loss I do have occurred many years ago in the Vietnam war when I stood right next to a twenty-man 81mm mortar unit that fired day and night at enemy targets. At that time, most people did not wear any ear protection. My follow-up conversation with Dr. Tolton was even more pleasant as she told me I could fly again, but she just wanted to see one more report. As my friend Bob Rennie says, "We are working our way back to the grave," so every day I can spend flying is a bonus. As I rose above the clouds on a flight back from Tofino a few days ago, I could not feel more thankful of Dr. Tolton's assistance in approving my conditions to fly again.

19

VANCOUVER PUBLIC LIBRARY

A Living Legacy

THE VANCOUVER PUBLIC Library is as old as Vancouver itself. In January 1869, J.A. Raymur, the manager of the Hastings Mill, established a meeting room and library for mill employees; it was later named the Hastings Literary Institute. The City of Vancouver was incorporated on April 6, 1886, the year before the first Canadian Pacific Railway transcontinental train reached the Pacific coast. In 1901, the City of Vancouver came to an agreement with American industrial philanthropist Andrew Carnegie to build a library at the corner of Hastings and Main Streets, on land provided by the city. The library opened in November 1903, and is now one of twenty-one branches of the Vancouver Public Library system.

Sally Warren, a director of the Vancouver Public Library Foundation, called me one day in 1989 and asked if I'd be interested in the library's story. She had heard about my work at the St Paul's Hospital Foundation and said that they were looking for someone to chair their foundation. We arranged to discuss it over lunch. I was not certain I wanted to do this.

Sally and her husband, Michael, were dear friends of mine. Michael and I had many business dealings in the early nineties, one of which unfortunately resulted in Nesbitt Thomson being sued by the Terry Fox Research Institute, of which Michael was a director. The lawsuit was ultimately dropped, but it caused a rift in our friendship for many years. We were able to reconcile a number of years later, when my daughter Tasha noticed him in a restaurant we were eating at and said, "There's your friend Michael." I approached him and gave him a big hug, and we reconnected after a long estrangement.

Libraries have always played a role in my life. When Bob Dorrance and I created a report on Canadian chartered banks for Nesbitt Thomson in the seventies, we relied heavily on the research facilities of the Montreal Public Library. The top floor of Nesbitt Thomson's office in Old Montreal (which is now the ultra-high-end Hotel Le St-James, where guests like Madonna and the Rolling Stones often stay) was a small library. The librarian was an avid reader who helped me put together the research report on Canadian Pacific that made my name in the investment business in the seventies.

The library was such an iconic institution, but I was not sure that libraries in Canada had the community support to raise money publicly. A lot of people feel that library funding should be covered by the city. Many Canadians find it easier to give to hospitals or universities than they do to libraries. So before I agreed to chair the foundation I decided to go and look at how people use libraries and why they matter. I soon saw that libraries attract people from all walks of life. When I looked up the staircase of the main library off the entrance off Georgia Street, I would see many lined up before 10 a.m., when the mad rush would begin. I was reminded of people lining up at Tokyo train stations, who hustle in the instant the doors open. The people who were streaming in those library doors came from many different backgrounds—students, veterans, businesspeople—and were of all ages. How could I not help? I felt that if more people read more, we would learn and make the world a better place. Libraries are like a trip around the world. They open your eyes to so many possibilities. On my fridge in Whistler is a magnet from VPL that says, "Free for all."

After I agreed to chair the foundation, Sally gave me a VPL mug with a lovely quote from Jorge Luis Borges: "I've always imagined paradise would be a kind of library." At the time, I said, "There is not too much awareness about the library, so we have much work ahead of us."

When I first arrived in Vancouver in 1979, the main branch of the VPL was at 750 Burrard Street. In 1995, it moved into a new Central Library building at Georgia and Homer designed by Moshe Safdie, who was a master's student at McGill when my father was a professor there. Safdie's thesis at McGill was the basis of what became Habitat 67, and one of his earliest designs depicted a group of houses, one on top of another, side by side. The new library is similar in design to the Colosseum in Rome.

I have a love for architecture, and at the time the Central Library was being built, I was building a beach house in Tofino that won two awards from the American Institute of Architects. The Central Library is very close to the Canadian Pacific Railway station and just down from Beatty Street, named after Sir Edward Beatty, who was president of Canadian Pacific Railway at the turn of the century. My history with Canadian Pacific had come full circle, and I was about to start a sixteen-year journey as chair of the VPLF.

I was an investment banker with a sense of history who had learned to give back. The library was something I would never give up on. The reason I stayed for so long is that I wanted to see it become a success and be recognized for the great institution it is.

In the early years, it was difficult to get support for the foundation from the public, let alone the library board itself. But because of people like Sally Warren and Paul Whitney, then the city librarian, we began to pluck away. Also key were Allan MacDougall, the cofounder of Raincoast Books, who loved to ski at Whistler like I did, and Lori Mathison, a prominent lawyer. While we saw many people come and go, this core group continued to press on.

I realized early on how important it was to focus on the cause and not the politics. While it may have been easier to raise funds for a bricks-and-mortar building, the foundation and the library wanted people to understand how early literacy programs like "Man in the Moon" could meet our individual community needs, especially if they were enhanced by fundraising for specific materials like the Aboriginal collection, and how people with sight impairments could benefit from a wide range of technological devices. I met many mothers and fathers who attended library programs with their children and saw how they benefited them. The year 2006 was a turning point for the foundation, when we brought together seven major donors to establish a story bus with children's services. In my office, I have a picture of Gordon Campbell, then mayor of Vancouver, sitting in the bus and saying thanks to me. The story bus presented story times, puppet shows, and singalongs at library branches throughout the city. Children's librarians could hop on the brightly painted van to visit preschoolers, their parents, and caregivers. The library and foundation recognized the need to reach youngsters who never had the opportunity to visit a physical branch.

I will always be grateful to Jeff Hollands, who runs a car leasing business, for agreeing to fund the story bus with me. He helped me find a van that the library could use. It may have not been a big-ticket item, but thanks to Salman Partners, Burrard Leasing, and the RBC Foundation, we had an attractive vehicle that gave us opportunities to both serve our library community and advertise our charity. Kids couldn't wait to see the van and the books the librarians were carrying. I've always felt that in charity work and giving back, it was important to focus on awareness, and the story bus was just that.

In the first ten years I was involved with the VPL, we raised about $4.5 million. Not a lot by today's standards, but it was a start. At the time, we were not able to track major donors, so we had to do something to move this thing forward. I could not stay on this road forever, but the Marines taught me to never give up. There was one major donor we did know, however: Canadian Pacific Railway, who donated $50,000 for the digitization of the historical photos the library owned. This was a natural fit for the donor as Canadian Pacific's history in Vancouver is as old as the city itself.

The first Vancouver Public Library building now houses the Carnegie Branch. I have often watched as Chinese Canadians, many of them seniors, lined up in the morning waiting for the library to open so they could read the latest Chinese publications. This library is now in a tough part of town in the Downtown Eastside, but this doesn't stop those citizens from standing in line to access its facilities. We used to have a health fair in the alleyways next to Carnegie to support good health and community stewardship for people who live in the surrounding neighbourhood. These small gestures show that the library has a soul and can move beyond books, and beyond its physical buildings, to engage more in community life. Vancouver's libraries have the potential to reach the community in a big way as each of the twenty-one branches has its own distinct ethnic and socioeconomic profile.

For example, the branch on Denman Street in the city's West End is named after Joe Fortes, a famous Black lifeguard on English Bay. The Joe Fortes library sits in an area known for its cultural diversity, with numerous restaurants, coffee shops, and bars, and not too far from the apartment on Comox Street where I lived for a short time prior to going to graduate school. Little did I know then that I would return to Vancouver thirty-five years later to chair the VPL Foundation. Like Joe Fortes, I found myself on the verge of something good to come.

Each branch of the library has a story and a following, which I was able to appreciate during the years of chairing the foundation. Take the Marpole Branch, close to where my daughters and grandchildren live today; it was named after Richard Marpole, an official of the Canadian Pacific Railway. The foundation raised $600,000 to support the new Mount Pleasant Branch, which opened in 2009. Mount Pleasant is a culturally rich area that includes many Indigenous community members. Some of the funds were used to inaugurate our First Nations storyteller-in-residence program as well as an expanded collection of Indigenous books and online resources. These materials were selected in collaboration with the Indigenous community. Catherine Evans, the chair of library, and I worked in collaboration to ensure projects like these all received sufficient funding to make them sustainable far into the future.

—

TEN YEARS after I became chair of the VPL Foundation, I came to believe that we needed to raise more money in a major campaign. We had to put the library on the mainstream of major fundraising initiatives, and we were not there yet. So to get the ball rolling, I decided to donate $300,000 in the BMO shares that I had earned when the bank took over Nesbitt Thomson. I did not designate the money for any particular project, but instead left it up to the board of the foundation to decide how it should be spent. (Those shares would have been worth nine hundred thousand today, but foundations have an unwritten rule of selling every share they receive early; I often wonder if that is a good policy when you're dealing with blue-chip companies.)

The library board decided to spend the money on opening a new branch in the recently renovated Hillcrest Centre, site of the Vancouver Olympic/Paralympic Centre during the 2010 Winter Games. After my donation, we were able to attract a number of key people. The executive director now, Jenny Marsh, and the new chair, Susan Knott, introduced us to John Montalbano, the former RBC executive who chaired the campaign. He put together an impressive campaign cabinet, which was responsible for the huge success of the fundraising effort that followed.

I am fully convinced that the next campaign for the library will be much larger than the first one. The St. Paul's Hospital campaign I chaired was a fraction of their recent campaign, for which I was a campaign cabinet member, which already has $275 million. It's important to plant the seed early, knowing it will grow. Jenny and I continue to work for the VPL Foundation to this day. She's a crucial part of the foundation who enabled us to take it to a new level. Whenever she called me to discuss a new project she wanted to fund, I could never say no.

The Terry Salman Branch of the Vancouver Public Library opened in October 2011, thanks to the city's Olympic legacy planning. It is part of the Hillcrest Centre; the building also houses various fitness facilities, including an NHL-sized ice rink and a swimming pool.

When I had the rare honour of having a public building named after me, I never forgot that the city had to approve it. Even more surreal was that Andrew Carnegie and I were the only persons who were alive when a branch or library was named after us. At the opening, the mayor at the time, Gregor Robertson, joked and asked me if I'd like another branch named after me, as the city had another one in the works. I was especially touched that this naming opportunity was recognition for my years of service to the library. As a dear friend once said, "It is easy to write a cheque, but hard to make the time commitment." The library honoured me in this way, and I am forever grateful. To this day, I still rank in the top five donors to VPLF, but more important than the money is what it did to enhance the library's programs; that is the strongest legacy.

The library has a stunning setting: beautiful Queen Elizabeth Park, a place where you and your children can read a book. A stone's throw away is Nat Bailey Stadium, a forties-style baseball field. On the other side of the library, you can watch a hockey game on the ice rink. Every time I visit, I think back to the day my granddaughters Amber and Naiya, two and four at the time, went there to look at the sign, which read, "Future home of the Terry Salman Branch." In my office in Vancouver, I have a framed picture of them holding hands in front of the sign; in the foreground is a reflection of their father in the window. Sometimes I go on the VPL website and read the comments about the branch, which are mostly very positive, unlike many other reviews on the internet.

Having a library branch named after you is kind of surreal. Even though I don't live nearby, I try to go there as often as possible, often with my grandchildren. If I request a book from the VPL I always ask to pick it up at that branch. Often my friends who visit the branch send me texts and pictures of themselves outside.

There are not many more iconic staff there than Adam, whom I got to know when the branch first opened in the fall of 2011. Adam was a full-time librarian and sat at the front desk in the middle of the branch. He conducted story-time when Amber and Naiya were very young. They used to have to stand on a box provided by the library to enable them to use their library cards. Adam still works there part-time. At Christmas, he makes a giant LEGO decoration encased in glass. I would bring the staff Lucky's Doughnuts, and I still visit them regularly. Libraries are the soul of a city. The VPL's latest branch, nə́ċaʔmat ct Strathcona, is the first public building in the city of Vancouver with a First Nations name, a long overdue recognition.

20

THE TOWN WHERE ROAD MEETS SEA

T HE SPRING OF 1979 was a golden age for independent dealers as they were about to be acquired by the banks. I had just
arrived in Vancouver and, after a few days at the Bayshore
Inn by Stanley Park, was staying at the Blue Horizon on Robson
Street. It was an old building and less expensive, but I had room
for my bicycle, which was my pride and joy: a blue Raleigh Carlton
professional road bike, handmade in Nottingham, England; you
have to apprentice for seven years to make the frame for this bike.

This was the second Raleigh I had owned; the first was stolen off the moving truck from Montreal to Vancouver. When this
happened, I called my father and asked him if he could buy me
another Raleigh professional bike, which I'd seen hung up in a
bike shop, if I paid him back later. He agreed, so it was only fitting
that I used the bike to visit the first place he worked after he finished his degree: Britannia Mines.

I was thinking of my father one day when I decided to ride
my bicycle from Vancouver fifty-five kilometres north along the
Sea-to-Sky Highway to Britannia. He had told me in those days
you had to take a barge from Vancouver to Britannia, because the

only roads to Whistler were narrow, treacherous logging roads; it only became safer after the new highway was built for the 2010 Olympic Games. Two years after my bike ride, the highway was wiped out by heavy rains and nine people lost their lives when the wooden bridge at M Creek was washed away.

My father arrived at Britannia in the summer of 1939 with a brand-new mining engineer's degree from McGill University. At the time, it was one of the largest copper mines in the world, and one of the longest-producing; it would produce copper and zinc concentrates for about seventy years. I'm not sure of my father's position at the mine, but he must have been a mining engineer or a mine captain.

When I got to Britannia, I saw that it had only closed five years earlier, in 1974. The concentrator and the mine buildings were shut and the only sign of life was the Mountain Woman Take-Out, a legendary eatery at the entrance to the mine site, owned by a woman called Lynne who has fought various developers and levels of government who wanted to kick her out of her location. I loved the place immediately and have been going there for more than thirty years now—the french fries are the best anywhere, especially with her malt vinegar.

I saw a phone booth at the entrance of the town. I called my father with my calling card to tell him I had cycled to Britannia, but unfortunately, he was not home to pick up the phone. Shortly thereafter, on April 26, 1979, he passed away. McGill University lowered their flag to half-mast to honour him. I called them and asked who had made this decision and why, and they told me it was at the discretion of the governors of the university and was not done very often.

Many years later, Michael McPhie and Bob Dickinson asked me to be honorary chairman of the Britannia Museum fundraising project, with the aim of expanding an existing museum to celebrate mining in BC. I agreed, as my father had worked there and mining had been a major interest of mine for decades. However, we were all aware that Britannia Mines had become one of the worst polluting mines in the world, with high amounts of cyanide pouring into Howe Sound. It was not a mine that the industry was particularly proud of.

A few years earlier I had met John Meech, who had been a student of my father at McGill and talked about him as his lifelong mentor. In their memoriam tribute to John Meech, UBC said, "While studying at McGill University, Dr. Meech was inspired by Professor Tal Salman, one of Canada's most outstanding mineral processing engineers, whose knowledge was described as 'genius level.' John came to regard Dr. Salman as a father figure in his professional life; it was he who inspired Dr. Meech to pursue the field of mineral processing."

John later became the head of the department of metallurgy at UBC. He had spent years working at Britannia, stopping the cyanide leakage into Howe Sound with what was known as the Millennium Plug Project. John lived long enough to see dolphins return to Howe Sound after a long absence.

So, when Michael and Bob contacted me, I called John and asked him to meet me for lunch. We talked about his vision for Britannia and other research projects he had in mind. Like John, Bob Dickinson was passionate about Britannia; he also lived close to the mine, in Lions Bay. He wanted the new museum to be a fun institution that could educate students, children, and the general public on the broader view of the mining industry.

Our goal was to raise $13 million. We had a desirable site overlooking Howe Sound with a small harbour and many attractive historical buildings, which millions of people pass every year on their way to Whistler. The other aspect we wanted the public to see was the soon-to-be-renovated concentrator building, a spectacular, twenty-storey structure hugging the hillside, with more than four-teen thousand panes of glass in its windows. This structure's form was appreciated by many, including architect George Christensen, a student of Ludwig Mies van der Rohe at Illinois Institute of Technology. George designed my house in West Vancouver as well as homes for many celebrities, including one heir of the Campbell's Soup Company. He even started designs for me on a house in Whistler with the same architecture as Britannia, which I loved, but which unfortunately we never built.

One of the first people I approached for this museum fundraiser was my friend Ross Beaty, who was an easy sell as he was already engaged in the project. As a mining executive and an environmentalist, he really wanted Britannia to be cleaned up and the site turned into a world-class museum. He pledged a million dollars and told me to go see Lukas Lundin, a billionaire mining entrepreneur. I went to Lukas's office, laid out the Britannia brochure, and told him about our vision. He liked the idea a lot, asked, "What did Ross give?" and matched the amount. They were not done yet; both Ross and Lukas ended up doubling the amount they had pledged, which is why the information centre at the museum, which houses a beautiful collection of mining samples that Ross previously owned, is now named the Beaty Lundin Visitor Centre. I was a messenger, and they delivered big time on their pledge.

Teck Resources was one of the few major companies that had their head office in Vancouver, and the only one until Ian Telfer was successful in moving Goldcorp there. Bob Dickinson got Teck on site and they ended up being among the top donors to the museum project. On the way back from the Denver Gold Forum that year, I had the good fortune of sitting next to Ian Telfer, who was then the chair of Goldcorp. Not long into the flight, I approached him on Britannia. He paused and said, "I will give you half a million dollars to blow it up." I said, "That would be impossible because it is a National Historic Site." He and Goldcorp gave us half a million anyway.

In the end, the museum was supported by many mining companies, as well the governments of British Columbia and Canada. The little village of Britannia is now a pleasant place to spend the afternoon. You can even have breakfast or lunch at the Driftwood Café or fish and chips at Mountain Woman. On a summer day, I often take my Harley-Davidson motorbike to Britannia to reflect on how far we have come with this museum and all the good this facility does in making people aware of the importance of the mining industry to Canada. My father never went back to Britannia, to my knowledge, and never really talked about it much. I hope he'd be proud to see it now.

21

TRIPS OF
A LIFETIME

SOME OF MY most memorable overseas trips have been with the mining entrepreneur Robert Friedland. My favourite Robert Friedland story began when I was crossing the street outside the convention centre in Cape Town, South Africa, in the 2000s. Salman Partners covered the old Ivanhoe Mines and most of Robert's other public companies, and we were both in South Africa for the Mining Indaba conference. Cape Town is one of my favourite cities in the world, and it's sunny and warm there in February, so I've happily attended this conference for many years. Robert asked me for my passport and said we were going on a trip throughout Africa. I had heard stories of people who got on Robert's plane and did not get off for a couple of weeks. It was my fourth and last trip with Robert—what he referred to as "jumping on the bus."

The "bus" was a Bombardier Global Express, a large-cabin business jet on which he entertained investors like no one I had ever seen before. Robert was a passionate presenter, and when he spoke at these conferences, there was always a sold-out audience. Conference organizers always made sure that Robert was scheduled for prime time. Other speakers did not have the draw he did.

He kept reinventing stories that would keep you on the edge of your seat.

We left Cape Town the day after the conference that year. Because we were on a private plane, we had to clear customs at Lanseria Airport. As soon as we were airborne, Robert realized that he did not have all of his luggage, so we had to go back to Cape Town and repeat the whole process. We landed in Kinshasa in the middle of the night. I had never been to the Congo, and was very excited. The airport was pitch black, and apart from the runway lights and the dimly lit immigration building, there was not much to see. In the Congo, when they take your passport, you don't get it back until you leave.

When we got to our hotel, Robert pointed out the holes on the outside of the building. The rebel forces in previous times had lobbed .50 calibre machine gun bullets and mortars across the Congo River. While Robert went to see the prime minister with Sam Jonah, another mining executive, the rest of our contingent went to see an ape rehabilitation hospital known as Lola ya Bonobo, the only sanctuary in the world for orphaned bonobo primates. Founded in 1994, it is rated the number one thing to do in Kinshasa. Many of their bonobos were rehabilitated after being found ailing of natural causes or being left for dead by poachers, who hunt them for their skins. This educational centre was a highlight of the trip and a nice break after the mining conference.

The next day, we headed for Marrakesh, Morocco. Later that afternoon, Robert suggested we go for a run through the city, where the locals looked on with some curiosity at these Westerners making their way through the winding, dust-covered clay streets. Dinner was at one of the best restaurants in the world. Before that, we had an up-to-date presentation on Ivanhoe Mines.

Robert finds and develops more world-class mines, which often start out as exploration plays, than anyone I know. Each time I travelled with him, I was always aware that he was onto his next discovery, just no one knew it yet. When I first went to Mongolia with him in 2009, it was already a discovery, but the size of the ore body was not well defined. As ever with Robert, it kept getting larger and larger as his exploration spending grew. At the time when most people would sell to a major, he would wait until he could prove there was more of a resource. From a research perspective, we always covered his companies with Ray Goldie, our senior base metal analyst who wrote a book on Voisey's Bay, one of Robert's earlier discoveries. We valued our independent research. One day on the plane to his mine in South Africa, Robert stood up in his aircraft and told his guests that he couldn't buy Ray Goldie; we valued our independent research, but not everyone did.

Robert, with all his persuasion skills, was very convincing and always loyal to us. One day he called me from Singapore and took a strip off me for allowing Salman Partners to take a small underwriting position in a company called Entree Gold that butted up to his Ivanhoe ore body in Mongolia. I told him it was a small position they were offering, but he understood loyalty, and I did, too, as I was a Marine, so I could appreciate where he was coming from. On my first trip to Mongolia with Robert, the Ivanhoe stock kept going up as we travelled; it was hard to say if Robert's presentations had anything to do with it, but I highly suspected it did. He made Mongolia fun for us. It's interesting to note that after Robert sold the old Ivanhoe mines to RTZ, who changed the name to Turquoise Hill Resources, the stock prices never reached the same historic level.

I first met Robert when I was with Nesbitt Thomson in the 1980s. My friend Peter Meredith was Robert's right-hand man in those days and helped me keep in touch with Robert and arranged many of our trips together on the "bus." They were educational experiences, to say the least. As a man so wealthy who did not need to work anymore, Robert put us to shame with his work ethic.

He was ahead of his time, and it was always a good time to go with Robert when he was about to discover something significant.

San Francisco has a special place in my heart as it was my address when I was in the Marine Corps during the Vietnam War. Every time I visit the city, I remember using this address as a way in my mind of actually living there. It's one of my favourite cities in the world, and I'm proud of my association with it. A few years ago, I was inducted into the Rick Rule Resource Hall of Fame at a mining conference there, an honour given to me by Cambridge House, who often hosted world-class mining conferences. There is nothing more beautiful, when you are in San Francisco, than seeing the fog rolling in over the harbour, engulfing the sunlight. When I entered the lobby of the Mandarin Oriental that morning in early 2018, it was sunny. A few minutes later, as I entered my hotel room on the top floor, the fog had taken over our entire building, beautiful in its own way. I emailed Robert Friedland and told him about the award and remembered the wonderful times we had spent together in San Francisco.

On the second of the four trips I took with Robert, we went from San Francisco to Fiji, then on to Brisbane in Queensland and finally to Kalgoorlie in Western Australia, where we attended the Diggers & Dealers conference. Diggers & Dealers is the leading mining forum in Australia. Kalgoorlie is a historic mining town and the site of the Super Pit, one of the largest and longest-standing gold mines, after Broken Hill, historically the most significant mining town in Australia. The Super Pit seems to go down for miles. You can watch the trucks come up from the bottom on a highway curving up from the valley floor—it's a sight to behold. During Diggers & Dealers, the whole town is converted to what it was like a hundred and fifty years ago during the gold rush era. With attractive topless waitresses wearing cowboy hats and not much else, the saloons around town attracted many characters, some attending the conference, and some just there to party.

As always, you never go on a trip with Robert without hearing him present the original Ivanhoe Mine story, over and over again. The funny thing is, it never gets old. Whether he is talking about copper as a green metal or the size of his operation, he engages the audience like no one you've ever seen. The next day, we were on the "bus" to Perth to get a first-hand technical view of Ivanhoe Mines from SRK mining consultants. We didn't spend much time in Perth, a city so far from anywhere else, but it was enough to see the beauty of the Western Australian capital's many parks and gardens. At Perth Airport, Robert took time to point out to us the R.M.Williams shoe shop, where he claimed you can buy the best boots in the world—and buy, we did. I still have a pair of R.M.Williams in dark brown kangaroo skin that I frequently wear. Robert was a very good salesman of local products. I think everyone on that trip came home with at least one pair of R.M.Williams boots.

Then we headed to Mongolia—my second trip there. We had dinner in Ulaanbaatar, and a day later boarded a Czechoslovakian-made plane, which appeared to be air-worthy, although I noticed that Robert was not on the same flight. I took comfort in knowing that the pilot was South African, and somehow, he would get us to the desert where the Ivanhoe Mine site was going to be. We stayed in a meticulously maintained yurt. It was a magical place to be, although we were warned that if we went out for a jog, we may never be seen again because the desert is endless and there are no roads worth putting on a map. We listened to the Ivanhoe geologists as they made presentations about the company. The size and scope of this mine was magnificent.

Robert's support of everything good that Mongolia has going for it was obvious on my trip there: "You have to a buy a Mongolian cashmere blanket that will keep you warm in the winter and cool in the summer." I bought two on his recommendation and he was right. When Robert left Mongolia the country did not do as well.

Robert didn't stop there. He now is building Kamoa, the second-largest copper mine in the world, in the Congo, which will produce 450,000 tons of copper per year. And in South Africa he is building the largest precious metals mine in the world and one of the world's largest platinum mines, which I saw nearly fifteen years ago just at the time a large Japanese investor bought the first tranche of what was going to become a $400 million investment! I don't see Robert much anymore, but whenever we meet, like we did at the BMO Global Metals & Mining Conference in February 2022, we exchange a big hug. When we embraced one another this latest time, though, we didn't say a word; it was different. It was a very emotional moment... he was so upset about the war in Ukraine, he almost appeared to break down. He showed the audience a picture of two Ukrainian children holding hands and waving to their dad, who was on a tank. We go back a long way, and I miss him and the days on the "bus." I have a standing invitation to visit Kamoa, which I hope to do someday soon.

—

THERE'S AN old saying that you will find gold and silver where others have found it before. That was the case in 2015 when I went to Bolivia to see the Silver Sand Project. When I asked the locals and my host what those steps in the distance on the side of a hill were, they told me the Spanish used them to access the silver mineralization on the property in the 1500s. Not too far from these steps were remnants of old buildings, one of which had a roof on it. Turns out the building was the old bank where the Spanish had made their silver coins. They mined this area for over a hundred years before moving on to nearby Potosí, which became the world's largest silver deposit. Today, this property is owned by New Pacific Metals Corp, with a market cap of around $775 million. Exploration is all about the geology and the commitment to prove up a resource in spite of the many obstacles faced by mining companies.

The Uyuni Salt Flat is one of the most beautiful natural reserves in the world, stretching over eleven thousand square kilometres at the foot of the Andes mountains. Rui arranged an early-morning flight to see this spectacular place, which was eye-poppingly gorgeous; sunny and warm by day but cool as soon as the sun drops down. We had a guide, but Rui, who is a geologist, had to correct him from time to time as he really understood the geological setting we were in. It was a place like none other where local people mined for salt and people who searched for unique natural settings went.

I visited China several times with Rui Feng to see one of the most profitable silver mines on the TSX, as I was an advisor for the company. You could eat off the floor of the mill building. While there one time, I visited Huashan, one of China's most sacred mountains. The stairs that line the stone trail were built over seven hundred years ago by a Taoist priest named He Zhizhen. This mountain is famous for its ledge, which people walk along to get from one part of the trail to the other, with a view of an eye-dropping valley thousands of feet below. I took a different route, but I had to go up to the ledge to see others who had more courage. As I climbed, I sensed that this place had so much history. I talked to vendors who made the trek up the mountain every two weeks, to offer hikers soup, tea, and other refreshments. While others took a cable car, we walked and walked to reach all seven peaks. My Chinese friends told even the older people who had taken the gondola that I was older than them but had climbed up by foot.

After climbing Mount Hua, we went on to Xi'an, the ancient walled city where the famous Terracotta Army sleeps. Chinese culture is so rich, and we spent several days learning and absorbing a small part of its vast history.

In 2014, Ross Beaty invited me to see the FIFA World Cup in Brazil. It was one of the most exciting sporting events I have ever been to. The sheer size of the event and the excitement it generated was something I had never witnessed. It was like the Stanley Cup Finals on steroids. Ross loves to use public transit, and for the final had us take the subway, which he said was the best way to go—and he was right, if your pockets weren't picked along the way. We saw three soccer matches in three different cities and sadly Brazil didn't win much. The excitement in the stadium was surreal, and wearing the wrong colours could put you in harm's way. I purchased an Argentina golf shirt at the gift shop as all the Brazil ones had sold. Ross was horrified: "You can't come into the stadium with that shirt on!" I watched the game with it in my bag.

—

WHEN YOU see the Indian Pacific in the train station in Sydney, you can't help but be impressed by the length of the newly washed cars that will take you across the vast continent of Australia. As you check in, you can sense that you are going on a real journey. As far as train trips go, this is one of the world's best, and *Conde Nast Traveler* ranks it as one of the top gourmet experiences. I can still remember the conductors on the platform with their Akubra hats and freshly ironed uniforms directing us to our platinum-class suite, which included a shower facility in our private compartment.

After I gave up Salman Partners' broker dealer licence, my wife and I decided to take this trip across Australia. Ross Beaty and Brad Cooke had just given me a farewell dinner at the Vancouver

Club. Ross said, "We could have filled the room twice over." Many of the people he had invited were in the silver industry, so he and Brad had prepared a gift of a hundred-ounce solid silver bar engraved with the names of my main clients, many of whom attended the dinner that night.

The Indian Pacific is a magnificent train, and crossing Australia on it is an adventure I had always wanted to experience. It is not a modern train; its old-fashioned cars were built years ago and recently refurbished to luxury standards. It only provides two classes of service—gold and platinum. The trip from Sydney to Perth in Western Australia takes four days and three nights. After forty years in two investment firms, I decided I had earned a break to enjoy the peace and serenity of the vast Australian landscape and figure out what I was going to do with the rest of my life.

The Indian Pacific is a photographer's dream, and I enjoyed spending hours learning to use a new camera with a telephoto Leica lens, something I had never had the chance to do. The camera lens was a gift from our dear friends Cherry and Robert Tunnock, whom we met at the resort called Dunk Island in the Family Islands when I was at Nesbitt Thomson in the early eighties. The maître d' had asked if we wanted to sit by ourselves or with another couple, and we soon found ourselves enjoying the company of the Tunnocks. We later spent a week with them in Melbourne when they were living in the Sandringham area near the ocean. We toured all of the sights of the city and, since Robert is a photographer, enjoyed countless hours visiting the art galleries and graffiti art that are a big feature in Melbourne. I was a young man who was covering the major mining companies in Australia, and oftentimes I strayed off the main streets in the downtown area and took the streetcars up and down Collins Street, where the head offices of some of the largest mining companies are located.

After the train departed Sydney and headed west across New South Wales, it was not long before we entered the lush green scenery of the Blue Mountains. We were served our first meal on the 4,352-kilometre journey, a gourmet feast with three meals a day prepared by the onboard chef.

Have you ever tried to sleep on a train? The constant sound of the car's wheels on the tracks helps you fall asleep easily. The sound rises and falls as the locomotive accelerates.

Now I wasn't thinking anymore about what kind of car or house I was going to build, or whether I should upgrade my 2003 Harley. It's strange, but my desire to consume started to disappear, even though I still enjoyed purchasing several new suits every year. I was at the stage in my life where I wanted to spend more time with people I liked but never really had the time for. I was raised a Christian, so I believed in what Dietrich Bonhoeffer said about how this life is not the grand finale, the next one is.

The Indian Pacific was filled with people with great stories to tell, and for once we had time to listen to a few, like the brother and sister—she being middle-aged and grieving the loss of her husband—who had decided to take this trip together. Then there was a young couple on their honeymoon, travelling across Australia. He was an officer in the Australian Army, so we had a lot to talk about. She was a medical doctor, who was burnt out from her job—and this was before Covid-19. This trip was a step back in time—there was rarely any cellphone service, so we could talk to all these interesting people without being interrupted.

At dinner, the conductor asked us if we were interested in stopping at Broken Hill, a mining town that's been one of the motors of Australia's natural resource economy since the late 1800s. Chris was not interested, but I got up at 6 a.m. to tour the town and its museum. Mining was why I first came to Australia almost forty years earlier, and Broken Hill brought me back to those roots. The town produced minerals such as gold and silver for over a century. Not far from the train station, we visited one of the world's highest-grade silver mines, which is still producing to this day.

The headframe on the mine is like a work of art, rising above the ground with its cables to support the men underground—lifting them up and down in boxes known as cages. Not too far from the silver mine is a striking monument to the more than eight hundred men who have lost their lives at Broken Hill since mining there began. It is inscribed with the names and times of death of all these men; the youngest of them was thirteen years old. To the miners, this is a sacred place. Beside this was a hall that celebrated the union movement in the mining industry with vivid, detailed portraits of every leader of the movement in Broken Hill.

We left the town the following morning and passed through the wine-growing region of the Barossa Valley on our way to Adelaide. It felt good to get off the train and enjoy this beautiful city on a bright sunny day. The highlight was touring the South Australian Museum, which is rich on the history of Australian paleontology.

Back on the train, two hundred kilometres north of Adelaide, we entered the ancient Flinders Ranges, the largest mountain range in South Australia. The ancient landscape out the window felt endless, especially when we entered the Nullarbor Plain, which means "no trees." That night, we had dinner under the stars in the outback town of Rawlinna. Not too far from this location is the town of Cook, which was named after a former prime minister—he must not have been very popular, because the town only had four inhabitants. They held an experiment to grow trees in another town nearby. The Nullarbor Plain is known for having the longest single railway track in the world, a 478 kilometres stretching across the vast landscape. The Aboriginal name for the plain is Oondiri, meaning "the waterless," as the average rainfall is approximately eight inches a year. Chris was not so fond of this part of the trip, but I was fascinated.

On the Nullarbor, the Indian Pacific was travelling at its highest speed of this trip, which really made you aware of the vastness of Australia. The Outback is a haunting place, especially on the Nullarbor. I was thinking how easy it must be to get lost out there. It's no wonder the British used it as a land of exile for criminals. The Nullarbor plain bakes during the day and cools at night, but soon the Indian Pacific had crossed into Western Australia and was on its way to Kalgoorlie, a gold-mining town I had visited many times before because it hosts the annual Diggers & Dealers conference. We arrived at three in the morning, so I decided to stay on the train.

The train then meandered its way through the lush green vegetation of Western Australia. The trees were much taller as we made our way towards Perth, where we spent five days at the historic hotel COMO The Treasury. Perth is a long way from anywhere, but we enjoyed this beautiful city immensely. The most notable buildings are the head offices of the many global mining companies based in Western Australia.

My love affair with libraries and trains started at the same time. Across the street from the hotel was Perth's stunning new library. I visited with my camera and took many photos of the stunning views and angles, with woodwork and carved vistas that made me want to stay a while longer. Using my Leica camera and all the lenses, I had to make sure I got every angle of this stunning building.

The Indian Pacific trip was over, but my love of trains would linger on. Someday I hope to take the Orient Express from Istanbul to Paris when they offer it again. There is also an Eastern Orient Express, which goes from Thailand to Singapore; that tempts me, though for some reason I have no interest in the Trans-Siberian Railway.

On the way back from Australia, we stopped in Bali and stayed at a magnificent resort called Amankila, a chain of luxury hotels. For both Chris and me, this was one of our favourite hotels ever. We went on hikes and toured the island. It was spectacular.

While we were sitting down enjoying the view, I received an email from the AME Roundup mining conference—the world's largest mining conference for premier technical mineral explorations—informing me that I had been given the Murray Pezim Award, one of the most prestigious honours in the mining field. It was wonderful to receive this news at the end of our trip. When they announced the honour, the AME wrote, "Terry Salman is the 2016 recipient of this award in recognition of his remarkable career in Canadian mining finance. Salman has been a leader in financing junior exploration and mid-cap to large mining companies over the past 35 years." I was particularly pleased by this announcement because I have spent my life following and promoting mining exploration companies, so it felt good to be acknowledged in this manner.

22

MEETING ESSENTIAL NEEDS

COLUMBIA STREET IN Vancouver's Downtown Eastside is filled with homeless people wandering around while others prey on those in need. The streets are dirty but sit among some interesting architecture. It was not as crowded as the nearby blocks of East Hastings, where many homeless people congregate to exchange goods, much of which the Vancouver Police say are stolen. The Essential Needs Foundation, the name created by my daughter Krista, would park its outreach truck on the quieter Columbia Street once every two weeks to give away a few essential items, such as sandwiches, socks, toques, and sometimes hygiene products. On a good day, giving away 152 Tim Hortons sandwiches would take less than an hour. Unfortunately, we had to stop this when Covid struck; the risk was just too great for Tasha and our other staff.

One of the philanthropists I admire is Brooke Astor, whose approach to fundraising inspired me. She gave back to numerous charities and once wrote, "Money is like manure. It should be spread around." She was awarded the Presidential Medal of Freedom.

I was able to start the Essential Needs Foundation by transferring some of the BMO shares I inherited as part of the transaction when the bank bought Nesbitt Thomson. We have used the proceeds of these dividends to do good things for those in need. For ten years, we continued to give out clothing and food—mostly Tim Hortons sandwiches as they are the preferred meal of our friends in the Downtown Eastside. We had many participants at this routine, called "the drop," including various corporate executives and even a retired Anglican bishop, James Cruickshank, a late friend of mine. No one left the drop without feeling good about what we had done. While it was a little gesture, it meant a lot to the recipients. It taught me that a few small things can go a long way.

We were not afraid of the residents, and they were not afraid of us. Sandwiches went quickly. When it snowed, it was even more challenging, as you could see how cold and hungry they were. The cold made us think how difficult it must be for them, and it made us wonder where they would go, or if they had a dry and warm place to stay, which we doubted. Yet in this brief hour and a half, we felt that we had made a difference, so we drove away feeling that we had done something good. We had a lot of willing volunteers from the business community and all walks of life. Theo, a successful businessperson, embraced this act of giving and was always asking when the next drop would be.

Being hungry is a difficult thing. It reminded me of my time in Vietnam—the few times we had a warm meal from the ship, myself and other NCOs and officers had to wait until the troops had eaten their fill. Sadly, the Downtown Eastside is one of the darkest, most drug-infested communities in North America, and it draws a lot of unfortunate media attention. So what could we do that would really matter? We took the most marginalized people and gave them food and clothing when they most needed it. A couple of hundred sandwiches and pieces of clothing every two weeks doesn't seem like much, but we got to be known around the area and people recognized us and gathered every week. Our volunteers were much appreciated; sometimes the visitors just wanted a hug from them. We all walked away with a sense of doing something special.

My friend Peter Meredith sometimes drove through the alleyways of the Downtown Eastside, dropping off clothing to the homeless community. In my garage, I have boxes of clothing that we have purchased in case a need arises on a cold winter day. Peter always said, "We could be any one of these people, Terry," and of course he is right. He always gives his change when asked by a homeless person.

The Downtown Eastside is not made up of only homeless people, but also veterans and caregivers and those in need who do have homes but have barely enough money to meet their basic needs. Even those who hang out outside the Carnegie library branch on East Hastings and Main Street often need help as well. This tiny library is a place where they can read books and other publications, even though they may go there hungry. Essential Needs is small, but we believe a small act can go a long way.

The *Globe and Mail* recently showed the faces of a hundred victims of the drug crisis on its front page. All had families, some had kids, and the pictures clearly showed them at a better time in their lives. One day, they were normal like you and me; then after one party, they were lost forever. Hard to believe? Take a look at those pictures. One block from our drop location on Columbia Street is a site where users can inject their drugs in a safe environment. While people say that safe injection sites are not a good solution, they are surely better than the alternative. You only have to take a look at the neighbourhood to see that.

Not too far from our drop location is the 625 Powell Street Foundation, the brainchild of Carl P. Vanderspek, who recently passed away. He created the facility with Dr. Julio Montaner, a one-stop shop for patients in the Downtown Eastside who needed medical attention and counselling. Carl bought a number of local buildings and catered to AIDS and HIV patients in the area who would not go to a hospital. Thanks to Carl and the support of the BC Ministry of Health, Dr. Montaner, who I know from my time at the St. Paul's Hospital Foundation, was able to create a safe facility not too far from Oppenheimer Park. I am not a board member anymore, as it is now a family foundation. And, sadly, Carl passed away recently. Dr. Montaner built out the 625 Powell facility as a showcase of what can be done to help marginalized people in need. The centre has an even greater role to play in reducing deaths caused by the opioid crisis—and of their 1,500 or so "clients," not one has died of an overdose to date. Known as the Hope to Health Research & Innovation Centre, Dr. Montaner's program has huge potential to reduce drug addiction–related deaths, and I intend to help my friend.

Essential Needs also continues to donate to other organizations, such as Christ Church Cathedral's Maundy Café, where they give out meals five times a week to hundreds of people in need. You would think that these are all homeless people, but they are not—they are people from all walks of life, seniors and young people alike. The church also has a bulk-buying program for people in the Downtown Eastside, whose budgets do not enable them to have enough food. In a small way, Essential Needs also helps the church as one of the donors.

—

AT THE dead end of a road leading down to Horseshoe Bay, motorcycles often park side by side at a spot facing the ferry terminal with a picturesque view of the harbour below. There is a no-parking sign, but most motorcyclists ignore it, and no one seems to be ticketing them. Across the street is a concrete circle sitting area, where people can take a break on the ride between Squamish and Vancouver and enjoy the beautiful waterfront scenery. Once, as I went to sit down myself, I noticed another motorcyclist with a leather jacket that said he was a veteran. Since I am a veteran as well, I asked him the obvious and told him I was as well. As we chatted, I mentioned that the Essential Needs Foundation had been supporting veterans through the Veterans Transition Network for many years, in particular for PTSD treatment.

After a long pause, my new friend looked at me and said, "If it was not for that program, I would have taken my own life." He told me that he had been at a point where nothing mattered when he found out about the program, which offered him the benefits of treatment and the chance to recover.

My encounter with this veteran had a profound impression on me at the time, and it continues to move me still. I hope I can see him again someday.

—

FAR FROM the picturesque Horseshoe Bay, a university student by the name of Michael Pratt called me from Langley, BC, and told me about a program that he and his sister Elizabeth had initiated called A Walk to Remember. They were going to plant a tree for every one of the Canadian veterans who died in the war in Afghanistan—158 trees. I do not know how they found me, but I was honoured to be asked to donate the cost of one tree. This living memorial sits in a beautiful setting, the Derek Doubleday Arboretum in Langley, where people congregate, particularly on Veterans Day, to pay their respects.

The core value of Essential Needs is to maintain the two meanings of our name by providing essential items to those in need. We also answer requests from many charities for good causes. Over the last decade we have given out a considerable sum of money that has managed to maintain a core group of funds, which we top up from time to time despite not having support from outside donors. It can be big or small. We were involved in several after-school programs with the library and community centres.

Among the recipients is Covenant House, a charity particularly important to my life and my daughter Tasha. They work in the Downtown Eastside and elsewhere. In their words, "providing love and hope to Vancouver's homeless and at-risk street youth, [they] help young people aged 16 to 24 who have fled physical, emotional and sexual abuse; those who have been forced from their homes; and those who have aged out of foster care." Tasha participates every year in Covenant House's Sleep Out to help raise awareness and money for their cause (which Essential Needs also helps fund).

During the Russian Invasion of Ukraine, my friend John McCluskey told me about a charity run by mining executive Stephen Quin and his wife, Bernice. Kingsway Foundation runs an orphanage and a refuge centre in Latvia to help refugees from Ukraine. We donated within days. Words cannot describe the good work they do.

There is nothing more essential than clean water, so when Lauren Brown Hornor approached me to support her charity Swim Drink Fish I couldn't say no. I was to help sponsor a gala in Vancouver and Toronto leading up to an art auction. On April 8, I attended the gala, and I wasn't disappointed. There were passionate speeches given about the need for clean water, and I learned that the related charity called Hudson Riverkeeper was founded by US Marines who came home from the Vietnam War and tried to fish in the Hudson River and found it polluted. An added reason for me to support this cause.

—

WHEN YOU have dinner in a private dining room at a first-class restaurant, you get a sense that people in the main dining area think something secretive is going on. That may have been the case when I met Megan Todd, who was one of the servers at Cioppino's restaurant in Yaletown. Megan had set up her workstation and was folding linen just outside the private dining room. She was dressed in a white jacket with a tie, standard wear at high-end restaurants. She has blonde hair and blue eyes and was twenty-one at the time. I introduced myself on the way out of the dining room. We spoke briefly, and she told me that she was a music student at UBC. It was customary in those days to give out a business card, but somehow I forgot.

The event I was hosting was a ritual called "the closing dinner," where investment bankers invite key players in a transaction to celebrate the completion of a long process. Megan remembered my name, and the next day called me. My assistant, Anne, picked up the phone. She put the call on hold and asked me, "Do you know a Megan?" I thought about it and said, "I don't think so." Just before Anne was about to hang up, I told her to wait and remembered that I had met her last night. I agreed to have coffee with her.

Megan told me that she had been accepted at Berklee College of Music in Boston, a revered institution that has produced over 350 Grammy winners, but she had no means of getting there and UBC was not her first choice. After a number of months of trying to find a scholarship or other financial means, I decided to help her realize her dream. She ended up writing a song for the hugely successful R&B band Earth, Wind & Fire, "Love is Law," that was produced by Sony Music. I had never been to Berklee until Megan went there. Unfortunately, I was not able to attend her graduation, but I did go to her wedding in Malibu, California. She also attended a number of events with me where she sang. She is now the mother of four children and still active in the music field. One day when I was in the Vancouver Club working out, someone approached me and said that he ran into Megan's mother, who had told him the story of my assistance to Megan.

—

IN KYIV, Ukraine, lovers often attach locks with their initials on them to a small pedestrian bridge known as the Lovers' Bridge. As I stood on this bridge on a cold sunny winter day, I reflected upon those who have attached locks there. As I walked back to my hotel, I felt thankful for the long wool winter coat Chris had bought for me a few years earlier, which was keeping me warm against the chill. As I approached the hotel, I saw a note on a church asking for clothing and other donations. On the spur of the moment, I went to the concierge in the hotel and told him I would like to donate my coat to the church. Sometimes giving is best done on an impromptu basis, when it comes directly from the heart and not from some glossy brochure or big description of what the charity does.

The concierge told me the church would be most appreciative, so I handed him the coat. When I told Chris about it later, she was upset at first: "That came from Holt Renfrew! Why not give them money?"

I told her that I was going to Cape Town, South Africa, right after Kyiv, and I wouldn't need a wool coat there. And money just wouldn't have the same impact; when it's as cold as it gets in in January in Ukraine, what you need is a good winter coat. She laughed and shook her head.

—

RECENTLY, I saw two people on a sidewalk in the Downtown Eastside, pulling a small red wagon like the ones children used to play with years ago. In the wagon were medical supplies and other items to protect the homeless from the fentanyl crisis. These two volunteers probably did not get much recognition, but I certainly noticed them. Volunteers are what drive most successful charities. Those who give their time and service most often do it in a selfless way. As an organizer, unless you reach out and find out who these people are, you will often miss their contributions.

I recently gave to a church in Vancouver on an impromptu basis to support the sixty or so volunteers who answered the call of making contact with people living in isolation due to Covid-19. Actions like these do not cost much, but sometimes even the simple act of reaching out by telephone can go a long way. These volunteers were doing something inspiring, under the radar. Over the past forty years, I've been active in numerous charities and volunteered at non-profit organizations to enrich my life and the lives of others. Many of the volunteers became my friends, and I still keep in touch with them today. It's not about how much money you give or how much time you spend doing these important tasks, but the difference they make in people's lives. Sometimes in larger charities, it is difficult to determine if your assistance really has an impact. If you dig deep enough, you'll find some good stories.

23

SINGAPORE

BY THE TIME this book comes to print, I will have served as the Honorary Consul General of the Republic of Singapore in Vancouver for over ten years. I never sought out this position, but I was honoured to be asked and to serve a nation that I have the utmost regard for.

The story began in February 2011 in Tojo's, one of Vancouver's best Japanese restaurants, where I met Koh Yong Guan, a life-long Singaporean civil servant who was then the non-resident Singapore ambassador to Canada. I found myself waiting a while for my guest, but then found out that he was sitting in the next booth, waiting for me. Luckily this misunderstanding didn't spoil our meeting. When I asked him what brought him to Vancouver, he told me that the sole purpose for visiting was to ask me on behalf of his government if I would take the position of honorary consul general (HCG).

I had met Koh Yong Guan a year or so before, after being introduced to him by David Brown, former chair of Ontario Securities Commission, whom I know from my days with the IDA board. David called me and told me Singapore was looking for someone in Vancouver to be HCG, as they had closed their permanent office here a few years before because the government could not justify the cost with so little trade happening between Canada and Singapore. The discussion was postponed when David Brown resigned from the HCG position in Toronto.

Singapore has an interesting history and is a financial powerhouse. Robert Friedland, who lives in the island city-state and knows a lot about it, told me I could not turn the position down. I had visited him and his wife there once, and their house had reminded me of my place in Tofino, built on stilts in a forest-like setting.

After some consideration, I decided to take on this position. It felt like another form of giving back, this time to a foreign government that I admired. So, Chris and I were off to Singapore for my first orientation. We decided to stop in Hong Kong on the way and enjoy the original Mandarin Oriental hotel for a few days. The Mandarin is known for its afternoon tea, which includes a set menu of classic Chinese tea that one must try. It was an interesting experience. I loved the old part of the city, where you could actually climb many stairs for a workout, as the city peers up from the hotel on Connaught Road. The views were spectacular from this unique running track. Compared to Vancouver, hiking in Hong Kong is very civilized. If you climb up high enough in Central, you can see the Victoria Harbour and Tamar Park.

After a few days, we boarded a Singapore Airlines flight on a brand-new Airbus A380, with our own apartment within. Singapore sees HCGs as extensions of their communication network throughout the world and treats them well; the staff knew who we were from the moment we boarded. When we arrived in Singapore, we met the consular staff who led us to the VIP section through immigration and then on to our hotel, the Shangri-La on Orange Grove Road. The hotel was in a park-like setting and not far from one of the best shopping districts in Singapore with some of the most expensive real estate in the world. One British tech executive, James Dyson, recently bought a penthouse apartment in Singapore's tallest building, once valued at a hundred million Singapore dollars, for S$74 million. It's hard to believe that in colonial times, this area was used for R&R by British soldiers based in Singapore.

I never get tired of going to Singapore. The city and its history fascinate me. Meticulously maintained colonial buildings sit alongside a wide array of modern architecture from famous architects such as Moshe Safdie, who designed the stunning Marina Bay Sands hotel, the new Changi Airport, and the Surbana Jurong Campus. Singapore's history also fascinates me, and I set out to find out as much as I could. Winston Churchill described the fall of Singapore in World War II as "the worst disaster and largest capitulation in British history." I wanted to understand what had happened and what made it so important. Both geographically and strategically important, Singapore has one of the most significant ports in the region. Its deep-water port was heavily fortified by the British, which is one of the reasons Churchill emphasized its importance.

I went to the National Museum to see what had happened first-hand. They have an exhibit known as Syonan-To, in which you can learn about the Japanese occupation through real people's stories, including audio recordings of the voices of people incarcerated by the Japanese forces. I also visited the Changi prison camp, where many civilians were held and beaten to death. The Sook Ching massacre claimed the lives of 25,000 to 50,000 ethnic Chinese.

We also went to the Ford factory on Bukit Timah Road, just twenty minutes from downtown by taxi, where life-sized mannequins show the British lieutenant-general Arthur Percival surrendering to the Japanese lieutenant-general Tomoyuki Yamashita on Feb 15, 1942. Not far from the factory is Bukit Timah Nature Reserve, where I go for a hike every time I visit Singapore.

In this national park, you can climb to the highest point of Singapore, the summit of Bukit Timah Hill, at an elevation of 164 metres. From this location, the Japanese army moved southward to announce that Singapore had been secured on Feb 11, 1942. I often take people for a hike on this trail and can only imagine what it was like for the people of Singapore on that day.

I am impressed by how Singapore embraces its history and creates public spaces like the nature reserve and various museums where you can understand what happened during the Japanese occupation. A plaque outside the Alexandra Hospital, for instance, describes how on Feb 14, 1942, the then British military hospital was attacked by Japanese troops, killing 250 patients and staff. The plaque points out that the attack was a retaliation against soldiers firing at the arriving Japanese troops.

Because of its strategic position at the crossroads of trade routes in Southeast Asia, and despite its tiny size, Singapore has always been important. It is a little-known fact, for instance, that most of the oil used in the Vietnam War came through the port of Singapore; of course, I was not aware of this when I served with the Marines during the war. Unlike many other countries that suffered during Vietnam and World War II, Singapore embraces its history and keeps it in perpetuity through museums dedicated to documenting the events.

In his poem "The Song of the Cities," Rudyard Kipling noted that Singapore's geographical location was important in bringing together the East and the West. He did not like the hotel room in the Raffles compared to those in European hotels, but he liked the food, nonetheless. He compared the climate to living in an orchard house. After a stranger told him the hottest month in Singapore is March, Kipling added wearily, "Yes, of course, let me lie in the place and let me drip."

The weather never bothered me, however, and I did not mind standing in line outside the Raffles' Tiffin Room for the lunch rush, where they serve the most extensive collections of curry anywhere. They had three buffet tables set up, with all the ingredients that go with Indian curry, including meat, seafood, and vegetarian dishes. The Tiffin Room opened in 1892; equally famous is the Long Bar at Raffles, where the drink the Singapore Sling was created by bartender Ngiam Tong Boon. The Long Bar has been restored, and they still serve peanuts with your drink and invite you discard the shells on the floor.

The architect of the Raffles Hotel was Regent Alfred John Bidwell, who also designed the Victoria Theatre and Concert Hall in Singapore. When Bidwell died, along with name and dates, his wife specifically noted on his gravestone: *Architect Singapore.* While Bidwell designed buildings elsewhere, his wife seems to have regarded his work in Singapore as his best.

—

ONE DAY not long after I had taken up the position as HCG, a woman who had worked at the former consulate-general office in Vancouver called me and asked me if I knew what I was getting myself into. "It's a lot of work," she said, "and I am available if you want to hire me." She told me there was enough work for several people, and I in turn confessed that I had no idea what was in store for me but would look into it. As it turned out, I was to become one of the most active Singapore HCGs in the world.

Historically, Singapore and Canada have had a strong relationship, and at one point they were connected by the Crown. Canada is one of the eight countries that supported Singapore on the day it declared itself an independent country: August 9, 1965. (I was not far away in Vietnam on that very day, but my mind was not on Singapore then.) Singapore Airlines used to fly direct from Singapore to Vancouver, and many Singaporeans immigrated to Canada over the years because of our similar educational systems, British history, common language, and the rule of law. Moreover, Canadian universities are a popular choice among young people in Singapore and often provide active exchange programs between universities here and there.

Every three years when my term came up for renewal from 2011 onward, I agreed to stay on, once again. The country treated me well and I felt an obligation to see it through. As most people know, when I get involved with an institution, I stay the course. This was a way of giving back to the people of Singapore and to those people who travel to Singapore and need our help. One day I had the honour of giving a baby girl her Singapore citizenship certificate in the presence of her parents. I have a picture of all of us in front of the Singapore flag. The parents were very excited and said, "We are proud Singaporeans." Some joys of life come with small efforts, and this is the part of the job I enjoy the most.

Another time, the Ministry of Foreign Affairs called me and asked for our assistance. It turned out that a Singaporean citizen had been caught in the crossfire between Vancouver Police and some drug dealers and been attacked by a police hound. The young man was just at the wrong place at the wrong time. By an unfortunate coincidence, he was here to train as a pilot at the same airport, Boundary Bay, I often fly out of. I had many discussions with him and tried to help as much as I could in getting legal and medical help. He told me he would probably never be able to fly due to his injury. Helping this young man was a pleasure, but in the end, I don't think I did much. Whether it's a charity such as St. Paul's Hospital or Vancouver Public Library, or volunteering as

HCG of Singapore, I look upon life as a way of giving back—and if you don't succeed, try again.

Singapore has one of the world's most successful economies, low unemployment, almost no homelessness, and is a very safe place to visit. I have behind my desk a picture of the prime minister of Singapore with his wife and me. His wife, Ho Ching, is chair of Temasek Holdings, one of the world's largest investment funds. I once told him at a gala that I wondered how many hands he had shaken that day. He replied, "Many, but they always made me feel welcomed and special."

When I started my role as HCG, I had sixty employees at Salman Partners, but by 2018, I had only three, and a nice office and consulate decorated with all the art pieces in my collection that Chris does not like. The pressure was on me to essentially resign from this position, but I kept it and am happy that I did. The Marines taught me to do more with less as the Corps always got the least amount of new equipment, but they considered this an emblem of pride. When I received the Order of Canada, the Minister of Foreign Affairs Singapore sent me a letter of congratulation: "Please accept my warmest congratulations on your appointment to the Order of Canada. This is a well-deserved appointment which recognizes your important contributions to Canada."

There are so many stories of us helping Singaporeans for over a decade. Before Covid, my Singapore consulate assistant, Lida, often visited older people in their homes to help them renew their passports or conduct other consular business. When I asked Lida why they don't just get their sons or daughters to help them with this, she replied, they just preferred her help.

On any given day prior to Covid, we would receive ten or so appointment requests, mostly from Chinese or Indian nationals, who require a visa to visit Singapore. It seems that everyone wants to go to Singapore, either to attend an international conference or to visit their many universities, which have a global reach. Since Singapore does not allow dual citizenship, we often have people visiting us to renounce their Singapore citizenship, usually reluctantly. I always tell them to think twice as it is very difficult, almost impossible, to get back. Singapore is among the countries with the highest quality of life in the world, and one of the highest life expectancies, so it's no wonder that people are reluctant to give up the benefits of citizenship.

I have travelled to Singapore many times, usually once or twice a year, and I often take Chris with me as she enjoys the country as much as I do. There are a few places in the world with as little crime as Singapore, and travelling by bus or the MRT (mass rapid transit system), adults and children feel very safe. Expats located in Singapore for business or consular positions are often supported by their governments or companies to compensate for the high cost of living. Singapore makes it expensive to drive your own car; the tax for your automobile increases with its value. This is part of a push to show zero growth and even reduce automobile traffic in the city. They are innovators in many other areas. At one point, for instance, they were importing water from Malaysia, but now thanks to their water-recycling system, they are actually selling their water to Malaysia.

The Singapore social network, developed under the leadership of Lee Kuan Yew, the country's first prime minister, is unique in the modern world. Through it, every employed person in Singapore is entitled to public housing managed by the Housing Development Board. This has increased much in value like other housing in Singapore, and therefore provides equity-based service for young couples and those entering the workforce for the first time. This has been tried in other parts of the world, but none has achieved the same success. In western countries like Canada, social housing is bought by the government to help in a modest way to assist the low-income population, but today it is almost entirely for homeless and marginalized people. Lee Kuan Yew's model has done a lot to prevent social unrest and unemployment in Singapore. To become a permanent resident of Singapore requires you to overcome a number of major hurdles, including sufficient financial wealth. In the years I've been HCG of Singapore, it has become increasingly difficult to become a permanent resident. Of six million citizens, around 1.5 million are non-residents; some work for global institutions, others are service workers who help keep the economy going. Not many countries have such a high percentage of non-residents.

One unfortunate incident that still haunts me today occurred in 2015, when a Singaporean woman passed away after a whitewater rafting trip near Canmore, Alberta. I was in contact with the appropriate authorities to verify the cause of her death and the transfer of her remains back to Singapore. It was a very difficult time to talk to her family as I was not able to comfort them face to face. I think they appreciated my effort. On a more positive note, they sent me a letter thanking me for what I had done. In these kinds of events, closure is very difficult.

Singaporeans are very proud of their country and go out of their way to use our consular services. One time, a lady wanted to sell her property and told Lida that she could have used a law firm, but she wanted to do this transaction through the Singapore consular office. A humbly dressed woman then visited our office to have me witness the document of the sale of her apartment building in Singapore.

—

I NEVER went into my career to try to do things in public service. Like most things in my life, I took, as Robert Frost said, the path less travelled.

My public service was to the governments of Canada and Singapore. My two notable contributions to Canada were my work as chair of the Investment Dealers Association of Canada, which sadly doesn't exist anymore, and my time on the expert panel set up by Jim Flaherty to make the case for a National Securities Commission. In total, these activities took fifteen years of my life.

Giving back takes many forms, and being HCG for Singapore is the only diplomatic role I have taken on in my lifetime, but one that I cherish. It is filled with challenges and never easy, but over time I've felt a sense of accomplishment by helping Singaporeans and those in need of assistance of visiting Singapore, because of what this country has to offer. It is hard to copy what Singapore has achieved as a nation. When you enter public service like this, you don't really do it for recognition, but as a way of giving back to the country and its citizens.

The first nine years of being honorary consul of Singapore was tricky enough, but the hardest part began when the Covid pandemic shut most towns and cities down in the spring of 2020. Staying open was a challenge, but with face masks, shields, and sanitizer, our small staff managed it. We helped people who were stranded and couldn't get home, as well as others who had lost their passports or were stuck on university campuses during the shutdowns.

More than a year into the pandemic, on New Year's Day 2021, I received a message early in the morning from my old friend Norm Keevil, telling me that the governor general had just announced that I was going to receive the Order of Canada. As you can imagine, I was deeply honoured. Among the many people who congratulated me was the minister for foreign affairs of Singapore,

Dr. Vivian Balakrishnan. I knew about the honour a few weeks earlier but had to keep it very quiet, only telling my family and a few close friends. It was the longest two weeks of my life, each moment seeming like an eternity. I wondered who may have put my name forward, but I am still not sure.

At the NHL game between the Vancouver Canucks and the Buffalo Sabres on March 20, 2022, a 13-year-old boy by the name of Graham sitting next to his dad, Bruce, asked me what I got the Order of Canada for. Taken aback, I struggled to reply, so he repeated his question, pointing to the snowflake on my Canucks jersey. Never having been asked that question directly, I told him it was for my charity work and my contribution to the mining industry. Somewhat lost for words, I showed him a mock-up of this book and told him a few specific things I think I did that helped.

I have no idea if Norm had anything to do with me receiving the Order of Canada, but I do know that he put forth my father's name for the Mining Hall of Fame, not once but twice. Because my father was an academic, he was never inducted; however, at the time, the committee looking at these matters told Norm they had never seen more letters in support of a candidate.

Six months later, one summer day in 2021, as I watched the early paddleboarders take off in front of my house on Stearman Beach in West Vancouver, I opened my email to find another message from Dr. Balakrishnan, this one passed on from the office of the president. It read in part, "My warmest congratulations on the award of the prestigious Public Service Star (Distinguished Friends of Singapore) in this year's Singapore National Day Awards, dated August 9, Singapore National Day." I had met Dr. Balakrishnan only once before, during a visit to Singapore in 2019. Like most things Singapore does, this was a class act that made me feel more connected to the country I have had the honour of serving for over a decade.

The invitation asked if I wanted to receive the medal in-person or not. It was the fall of 2021 and in the middle of Covid so I had to think about this for a day or two. Chris immediately said she was not going simply because she was worried about Covid and the stress of travelling in those times. I set out to go in person to receive this prestigious award. It was the least I could do, even though travelling was risky. At that time, gatherings in Singapore were limited to two people, which convinced Chris to change her initial reaction and join me.

The ceremony was elegant but without guests. I received a medal in a leather case from President Halimah Yacob, Singapore's eighth and first female president, who had just been handed it by a military aide. It was a brief encounter, but I couldn't help but notice how elegant she looked; the only thing I said to her was, "Nice to see you again," to which she nodded. After this very brief but special ceremony, Chris and I went for dinner at the Tiffin Room at Raffles to celebrate. As luck would have it, the restrictions had just been loosened to five people, so I was able to see some old friends too.

—

TODAY, ALBERNI Street in Vancouver, where our HCG office is located, is home to some of the most luxurious retail brands in the world, Prada and Tiffany, Hublot and Vacheron Constantin. It was not always that way. In fact, when Chris and I built our home in West Vancouver, Alberni was just an average street. The only thing still remaining from those days is Joe Fortes Seafood & Chop House around the corner on Thurlow Street, where horse-drawn buggies used to park when the city allowed that type of transportation. There was a horse often hitched there named Ed, and Chris would always give him carrots or apples. At that time, we lived in the Carlyle, a rental apartment building with a bronze statue of a doorman that is still there today.

There were no notable shops on the block back then, except a Chinese restaurant called Shanghai Chinese Bistro that people flocked to day after day. You can always tell a good Chinese restaurant by the number of Chinese customers in it, and Shanghai was full of them. They were known for their famous noodles, made by a chef who would throw the dough up in the air over three feet high to demonstrate his noodle-making skills. It was a scene I've yet to see since. We even had Chris's sixtieth birthday party there.

How fitting that I would come back to that street to our present office many years later. It hosts the memories of my entire life, from the Marines to the present. The many beautiful art pieces include a painting of me, which my wife dislikes very much; the Singaporeans seem to like it, though, and often want to have their pictures taken in front of it.

24

RETURN TO VIETNAM

IN 1989, ALMOST 25 years after I left Vietnam, I went to the opening night of *Miss Saigon* at the Theatre Royal Drury Lane in London with my wife, Chris, and my daughter Tasha. When I asked them recently what they remembered about that play, Tasha said, "the opening helicopter scene," and Chris said, "that gunfire where the main character took her life." I had not seen a single Vietnam War movie or musical or read a book about the conflict before that evening. It was a time too painful to remember, but for some strange reason, I found myself really wanting to see that musical. Perhaps because the male character was a sergeant in the Marine Corps like I was. The helicopter Tasha was referring to was lifting off from the US embassy during the fall of Saigon, as the last Marines at the embassy were evacuating the last civilians to leave the country. I just wanted to see the last moments of the Vietnam War played out on the stage.

Not too long after that trip to the theatre, I found myself sitting in my office, reading clipping after clipping from the newspaper showing all the battles we had fought in various places in Vietnam, all of which were later taken over by the Viet Cong: Hui, Da Nang,

Chu Lai, Khe Sanh. I still remember how sick to my stomach I felt, like I had an ulcer. No one in my office understood as they were all Canadian. At Khe Sanh alone, the Marines had 155 men killed and 425 wounded, in one of the deadliest battles in the Corps' history.

One day in 1997, the writer Peter C. Newman asked me to have lunch with him, so he could interview me for his new book *Titans: How the New Canadian Establishment Seized Power*. At the time, I was fine in my skin, a prominent investment banker with lots of friends and a deal flow that was impressive. But Peter didn't want to talk about Salman Partners or my fundraising, but my time in Vietnam. For three decades, I had not discussed it with anyone, certainly not a writer. Like many of the veterans described in the recent documentary series on the war by Ken Burns and Lynn Novick, I refused to talk about it, went into hiding, pretended everything was OK, and got on with my life (they deliberately chose no famous people in this documentary, to get a first-hand view). It was not a time I wanted to revisit. I was nervous over lunch when he started asking me questions; I thought I would never be talking about Vietnam again. Bringing back these painful memories was not something I was interested in, but I had so much respect for Peter that I decided to do it.

Five years later, I was in Washington, DC, on a business trip when I suddenly decided I should go and visit the Vietnam Veterans Memorial. I hadn't come to town for that purpose, but it had been on my mind for years. So I left my colleagues drinking and having dessert, hopped in a taxi, and went there; I got out at the National Mall and made the short walk to the Memorial Wall. It had taken me thirty-eight years, but I finally found myself staring at the black granite memorial carved with the names of the US servicemen who died in Vietnam. I was terrified the whole time that I would find the names of fellow Marines I had served with. Thankfully, I didn't.

The Memorial Wall is controversial. Some veterans love it; others find it too sombre. It reminds me of all that we lost, and that somehow, I came back unscathed, at least physically.

This past Memorial Day, I listened to a Marine playing taps there, and it brought shivers to me and caused me to tear up. As the bugler started the sweep of the memorial and the morning sun rose in silence, he started to play his haunting music. The Vietnam War memorial that we waited so long to see became alive in the morning dew, and quiet.

As I watched, I asked myself, Why did it take so long to have this memorial? It took a twenty-one-year-old Yale student named Maya Lin to bring the design to life and create a place for us to pay our respects at eye level to the 58,320 names on the wall, a number which does not include the many more that were wounded and scarred for life. The war is still fresh to all those affected; and unlike older wars, many of us are still around to remember. Veterans continue to suffer much more than the general public from homelessness and suicide.

In 2015, fifty years after I left Vietnam, Chris and I decided to go back to visit the country. We decided to visit Hue, the site of one of the fiercest battles of the war, during the 1968 Tet Offensive. In this now quiet place, I saw where half a century earlier the Marines assaulted the Dong Den Gate at the Citadel, the bullet holes on the wall left untouched from the carnage that took place there. The 4th Marines—who were originally based in Hawaii, like I was—suffered 147 deaths and 857 wounded in the battle. One of them could have been me, but for some strange reason, I'd served in Vietnam two years earlier. It was a sobering thought.

I paused and said a prayer at the Citadel.

The trip to Vietnam was a trip I never wanted to make. The war was in the past, and for a long time I hadn't wanted to relive it. It was only when I started to talk about the war and see movies about it that I became convinced that I should confront its legacy. Seeing the Viet Cong tunnels only reminded me of how hard they fought to win the war, no matter how long it took. We have such a short-term memory of the country and the conflict, but the Vietnamese don't. As we left the country, I finally felt at peace in a way. The economic powerhouse that Vietnam has become was evident everywhere, if by nothing else than the change from bicycles to motor scooters and motorcycles. The country and its people are successful and thriving now, as people everywhere should be.

When I told Jill Koshure, my old girlfriend from my Calgary days, that I had just visited Vietnam, she asked me why I would go there. It turned out that in all our time together, I had never mentioned that I was a veteran who had fought in a war. I didn't even know that I was keeping these things inside, but I guess I was, and it took me fifty years to address them and come to some sort of closure.

25

A DEEPER
VOICE OF GOD

W HEN I READ Richard Rohr's excellent book *Falling Upward*, I recognized my own life. Like Rohr, I focused the first part of my life on providing for my family. In the second part, which started in the 1980s, I was able to do good works for others.

Salman Partners was blessed with many talented people, especially in the period where the economics of the broker's business were positive for small dealers. But even later, between 2000 and 2011, the company participated in over four hundred transactions and in all accounts was a business success. All this financial success allowed me to step back from my day job and spend more time giving back.

Rohr talks about how the first half of his life was like falling, and that before you can be found, you have to be lost. For me, the falling was the deaths of my parents and a divorce, three events that occurred one after the other between 1979 and 1984. In that last year, around the time my mother was on her deathbed in Montreal General, the same McGill University teaching hospital where my father had died a few years before, I backed my car into a motorcycle parked behind me on Robson Street. Fortunately, no one was on it and the damage was minor. I lost my girlfriend at the time because I was still dealing with the grief of losing my parents. This series of events was what Rohr referred to as the first half of life; the second half begins when you hear "a deeper voice of God." Like many other people, I found myself contemplating my own mortality and what I was going to do going forward.

I am now at a point in my life where I am looking for new opportunities to help people in need, through Essential Needs or in other ways. Recently, I had the opportunity to donate to the purchase of an electric cargo tricycle to the VPL main branch, a green alternative to help librarians reach out to various branches with books and services. At the same time, one of Essential Needs' charities, the Maundy Café, was serving hot meals five times a week to anyone who wanted one, not just the homeless, but seniors and others who do not have enough food to eat. Our commitment was to provide seven hundred meals a week to those who live close by.

But I always have a set of rules when it comes to fundraising. When I started to raise money for St. Paul's Hospital in 1989, I was governed by one single rule: keep your costs low as a percentage of the revenue raised; my rule of thumb then was 15 percent. I learned that principle not from fundraising experience, because at that point I had none, but from my business experience and my time in the Marines. At Nesbitt Thomson, I worked for Brian Steck, who reinforced the need to be frugal. We flew economy and stayed at modest hotels. Steck was a hard-nosed businessman and the president whose job was to keep costs down. He even hired Heather Reisman as a consultant and advisor to make the company more efficient. That's why at St. Paul's, I felt comfortable working in the low-cost environment so similar to my background. In the eight years I was chair, we raised approximately $36 million, which in today's terms would be closer to $80 million. But our costs were minimal, and most went to the bottom line.

US Marine Corps Recon recruits learn how to survive on plants and snakes. To quote the motto of the 1st Battalion, 4th Marines, "Whatever it takes." My frugal background goes back even further than my time in the Marines. My parents had six children, and money was tight. We usually had one pair of shoes and a huge Christmas present would be a pair of hockey skates because we were only allowed one of anything. Later in my life when I started to earn good money, I developed the strange habit of buying two of everything.

At Nesbitt Thomson in the seventies, most of us couldn't pay our American Express bills. While we cut personal costs in other areas, an Amex card to us in those days was a coveted symbol of success. My card today says I am a member since 1972, which I still consider a real accomplishment. We had to live within our means, but Nesbitt Thomson was a blue-blood firm and what we lacked in profitability we made up for in blue-chip accounts like Power Corp and TransCanada Pipelines. We were the first Canadian dealer to be a member of the NYSE and at one point had a large New York office.

I was a director of the Prostate Cancer Research Foundation of Canada for six years. I didn't really know anything about prostate cancer at the time, but it seemed like a good cause, and we solicited funds locally in BC. Our major role was to raise money for the foundation and put on a fundraising breakfast every year; corporations who were clients of mine sponsored it and took a table. Over eggs and coffee, attendees would hear from a group of world-class researchers from UBC, to increase awareness of prostate cancer. The standard for detection of this common cancer is the PSA test, which we provided easy access to for as many patients as we could.

There is an old saying in British Columbia, that you go to university to get a degree, you go to BCIT to get a job. On June 18, 2009, I received an honorary degree from British Columbia

Institute of Technology (BCIT), BC's largest post-secondary school. In speaking to the graduating class that year, I tried to make the point that what they learned at BCIT is very practical and will be in great demand in the years to come. As the labour shortage that we anticipate in the decade to come arrives, what remaining jobs are available will require specific training and specialization of tasks. Not just nursing degrees, but all kinds of technical skills that the graduates are learning. After a number of high-fives, I encouraged them to never give up. I was fortunate enough to have my family in the audience, and even Megan Todd, who came up from her school in Boston. Today, I am on the campaign cabinet of BCIT, as the school embarks on its first major campaign.

The new bike path in Pacific Rim National Park Reserve is a magnificent paved road that winds its way through the forest from the entrance of the park to the town of Tofino. Some people believe it was built at great cost by the federal government because Prime Minister Trudeau loves Tofino. As I made my way home I noticed a cyclist trying to overtake me at high speed; unbeknown to me, he was actually trying to catch up to me, which wouldn't be hard to do. As he came within feet of me, he said, "Hi Terry." It was Pat Wolfe, who worked for me more than thirty years ago as an investment banker in Vancouver and is now a BCIT professor. Pat epitomizes what BCIT is all about: understated, smart, and caring, someone who takes a keen interest in his students and goes the extra mile to see them succeed. He clearly wanted to catch up, which we did at my place over tea later with his wife.

BCIT graduates more nurses than any other institution of higher learning in British Columbia, and BCIT-trained nurses were front and centre in the fight against COVID. In my first hot yoga class after the pandemic, I walked up to the instructor, Regina Zhan, and we gave each other a big hug. I took up yoga to deal with stress and at the most challenging period of my business and charity work was going a hundred days a year. When I started yoga, Regina worked at Yoga in Yaletown behind the desk. Now her classes are always sold out, as we acknowledged as we eyed the jam-packed room. Many in the class are BCIT-educated health-care workers who work in St. Paul's Hospital just up the street. One of her colleagues, I'm told, is teaching now at BCIT.

One of the more interesting fundraisers I've ever attended was in London on Sept 21, 2016. My friends Amir, Arash, and Rosalind Adnani, who are connected to the Vancouver art community, arranged for a big batch of Canadian art to be auctioned at an event for World Alzheimer's Month. I bid on one of those pieces, by Gordon Smith, a well-known Canadian artist who recently passed away, that was being displayed at Lancaster House, Queen Victoria's fondest residence, after a reception at Canada House on Trafalgar Square. Not only was the art expensive, but the freight to and from London, and the duty we had to pay to bring the Canadian art back to Canada, added hugely to the cost. But sometimes, you go a long way for a good cause, and there are not many causes that are more significant than Alzheimer's in our world today with its rapidly aging population. The painting, from around 2016, is like nothing Gordon Smith's ever done before, with contrasting colours of black, white, and blue revealing features that resemble a woman. He lived to one hundred years old and produced this piece near the end of his life journey.

People ask me who my role model in fundraising is, and I always answer "Audrey Hepburn." At the peak of her career, after winning the Academy Award, she retired from acting and dedicated her life to UNICEF, where she was an ambassador for many years. A few years ago, at the Vancouver Tiffany store, I showed my granddaughters the rare Tiffany diamond that Hepburn wore in the movie *Breakfast at Tiffany's*; it had only been shown outside New York City one other time, in Hong Kong. The way she used her fame to accelerate her fundraising commitments was very inspirational. When you look at pictures of her when she was on her UNICEF pilgrimages, you won't recognize any notable jewellery.

Sitting next to me on the table in my home where I wrote most of this memoir is *On Desperate Ground*, a book by Hampton Sides that my friend Brian Kennedy gave me last year. It is about the Marines at Chosin Reservoir, the Korean War's greatest battle. Brian is a mining executive who lives in Reno, Nevada. He is one of those people who I never really got to spend enough time with because I was so busy with my investment business and charity work. We have a lot in common; he was in the navy and is a graduate of Annapolis. In a note he put in the book, he acknowledged the sacrifices I made by being drafted to go to Vietnam. At this stage in my life, I want to spend as much time as possible with people like Brian, who made a simple act of kindness in sending me a book he knew I would appreciate. It means so much to me, as do his many phone calls. When it was announced that I was to receive the Order of Canada, he was one of the first few I called to share the good news.

Going forward, I have no idea which charities I would like to support as there are so many good causes, and this pandemic has made it even more important to give back. There are few charities that are not worth supporting. I am, however, convinced that I should contribute as much to charity work as possible, and what we give is not always about money but what we do to make the world a better place. Talking to friends like Brian helps create a positive frame of mind and positive energy, which we all need to move forward. And I now have the time to devote more energy to looking for good causes and ways I can help. Jeff Bezos said that the best thing you can do is wander, and from that will come the most creative ways to grow. Some of the best ideas I've come up with came to me when I was riding my bike.

People ask me which charities they should support, and I often answer, the ones doing work around climate change. There are a number of issues affecting Canada, and for that matter, the whole world. It is hard to say which issue is most urgent, but as a famous Grammy Award winner said, "There is no such thing as a bad cause, so support them all."

It is hard not to support charities that help to prevent drug-related deaths, of which there are now close to three thousand in Canada every year. One of my friends, a prominent doctor, supports reducing these deaths by administrating safe drugs, a controversial but certainly worthwhile cause. Another major issue facing Canada that could benefit from more giving back initiatives is Indigenous support. Recently we contributed to a scholarship fund for Indigenous students. As Deputy Prime Minister Chrystia Freeland said, the best thing we can do to help our Indigenous people is to support Indigenous prosperity, in areas like education and job opportunities. I like that idea a lot.

In my office is a lavender plant that commemorates the official ground-breaking of the new St. Paul's Hospital. I was on the campaign cabinet, which was a huge honour because we raised more than $225 million, which will go down as one of Canada's largest hospital campaigns. It took many years of committed planning by so many people to reach that goal. The cabinet sent me a packet of lavender seeds, which I planted, and which continue to grow. It is a reminder that charity often starts from a small seed and grows to an unimaginable size over time—do not give up on a good cause, the initial reject does not mean forever. Ask a potential donor once, but work on it if they say no. You'll be surprised at the outcome if you are patient enough.

—

THE MARINE Corps instilled the core of my value system, along with my parents, who were of course paramount. The Marines taught me that it's not about you, it's about the Corps. You're just one small part of something bigger. It's so hard to get that designation and such a sacrifice to be called a US Marine that when you achieve it, you never forget it. Loyalty's a big part of it: Semper fidelis—always faithful. So, faithful to the organization, faithful to your friends, faithful to the work that you do. And don't cancel. Marines don't cancel meetings or anything like that. If you have to be somewhere, you have to be somewhere.

I was telling my granddaughter the other day that the only thing I didn't like doing was jumping out of a helicopter on a rope. If I could find a way to go to sick bay on that particular day, I told her, I would. This came up because she has a fear of ending up in a bad place when skiing, even though she's a very good skier. I was trying to tell her that I had the same phobia in the Marines but I got over it. It was an interesting discussion to have with a ten-year-old.

The Marines take care—they do things that have a lifelong impact. They always go back and get their dead, even when there's a risk that they'll get shot themselves. That's a profound way of teaching you loyalty. What's the meaning of life? For me, it's giving back. You can collect things, you can have cars, you can have planes, but what can you do with your life that makes a difference? You can't just focus on yourself. A friend of mine just died. He dedicated 25 percent of his life to civic activities. I don't know what percentage I've spent, but I'm always believing in new ways. My New Year's motto this year, which I've barely told anybody, is to help as many people as possible, in whatever way possible. Because how many years do I have left? Five, six, ten, whatever. In business, in charity work, that's something I want to do.

As a friend of mine says, "To be continued..."

AFTERWORD

URING THE LAST two years through Covid, I withdrew to a place I never thought I would ever go. I always thought of myself as an outgoing person, but I started to doubt my former self. As an extrovert, not being able to talk to anyone, being with only my wife, and distancing myself from my children and grandchildren was very difficult. Writing this memoir in many ways kept me from falling into a state of depression.

"You are not the person you used to be, Dad," my daughter Krista said to me one day. She was right—I had gone from hosting dinner parties for fifty people to sharing dinner with my wife, Chris, and my biweekly call with my friend Keith Lambert. Krista sent me a book for Christmas by the novelist Stephen King on writing. It inspired me, and I began to walk downstairs to my basement every day and write a few pages on a two-hundred-year-old table that survived the 2018 flood.

As the winter dragged on, I continued to write at my place in Whistler, mostly solo. But like the Vietnam War, I can say that I've seen the best of my life, and the worst. Just as I thought we were getting over the worst wave of this pandemic, another one arrived. I read Albert Camus's book *The Plague*, in which he said that the pandemic brought out the best and the worst in people. One day, that plague just went away.

Two years of not seeing family other than my wife made me feel like these are the big moments of loss. The recent withdrawal from Afghanistan and the collapse of the government there brought back sad memories of the fall of Saigon. When I thought it could not get any worse, eleven US Marines, plus two other US serviceman, and over a hundred Afghan civilians, were killed in a suicide bombing at Kabul airport. One of those Marines reminded me of myself: Marine Sergeant Nicole Gee, who was, according to the *New York Times*, meritoriously promoted to sergeant ahead of her peers at the young age of twenty-three, the same age I was promoted to sergeant in Vietnam (both before four years in the Corps). Just as I was reading this story, my editor, Amanda, sent me a text asking how I was doing. The sadness I felt in looking at the bios of those who had died brought back so many hard memories.

In a trendy restaurant called One in the Yorkville area of Toronto during Covid, I took John McCluskey and Pierre Lassonde, one of Canada's greatest philanthropists who has given more than $100 million to charity, to lunch under a tent outside. Toronto was still under a lockdown. I wanted to thank both of them for all the help they have been to me. They were among the first people to congratulate me on receiving the Order of Canada. The conversation was upbeat, and I was so happy to be there with them. Years ago, in the early 2000s, John and I did one of the first financings for his company, Alamos Gold. We papered the transaction on my dining table on a Sunday, and the following morning I told my lawyer not to change the terms as we had a firm deal. Alamos went on to become a 400-thousand-ounce-plus producer of gold with a market cap of almost four billion dollars. John said after that lunch that we were two of his best friends. It was such an honour to be there with them.

—

ON A cold and wet Friday evening in December 2021, I received an email from the duty officer of the Ministry of Foreign Affairs of Singapore informing me that a Singaporean had been reported missing on Whistler Mountain outside the ski boundary area. Thirty-two-year-old Wen Yi Toh lost contact with his friend Kevin at around one thirty in the afternoon of the seventeenth. Environment Canada had a severe weather warning in place that evening calling for fifty centimetres of snow in Whistler, and winds of up to a hundred kilometres an hour.

At 10:17 p.m. that evening I received an email from the missing snowboarder's sister asking for my assistance. Shortly thereafter, I called the Whistler RCMP 911 line and reported a missing person. An officer called me back and gave me some information, including where Wen Yi was last heard from and the area they thought he may be. Whistler Search and Rescue had already started a search along with the Whistler Blackcomb Ski Patrol, but they had to call it off due to the weather. In the morning of Saturday, December 18, I called Steve LeClair of the WSR, who told me three snowmobiles and one ATV were already going up the mountain. A helicopter soon followed, but they had no luck finding Wen Yi. But Steve gave me one piece of hopeful news: there were fresh tracks in the deep snow (these later proved to not be from the Singaporean). That evening, the sky was clear. By then, I had become the liaison between search and rescue and the family, mainly Wen Yi's sister. I passed the hope that Steve had given me along to Wen Hui. We went to bed hopeful; I said a prayer and so did she.

That evening, Steve told me that WSR had asked the Canadian Forces at Comox, some three hundred kilometres away on Vancouver Island, to help with the search. They were pulling out all the stops. A Royal Canadian Air Force aircraft had searched the area but couldn't see the missing boarder—though later he would tell us that he saw them and was about to lose hope when they headed back to Comox.

On Sunday morning, December 19, from my house in Whistler, I heard a helicopter heading over the mountains. Steve called me a few hours later to tell me that this time the WSR helicopter had been successful in finding the snowboarder, picking him up and flying him back to a clinic in town, approximately forty-eight hours after he was last heard from. I passed this news on to the relieved family.

The helicopter crew had to punch out the door to put the injured boarder in the aircraft. Wen Yi was hypothermic from falling in a waterfall after he got lost. But he had used his military training to build a snow pit, line it with sapling branches, and shelter in it. He said he had started to lose hope just before he was rescued.

That afternoon I joined Wen Yi's friend Kevin at the Whistler clinic as Wen Yi was being put in an ambulance for a trip to Lions Gate Hospital in Vancouver. To quote Shakespeare, "All's well that ends well."

And my time helping Singaporean snowboarders was not over. On March 3, 2022, my assistant Lida received an urgent request from a young female snowboarder at Whistler who had lost her passport on the mountain. She needed a document of identity that would allow her to return to Singapore without a passport. The problem was that she was still in Whistler and her bus was picking her up at her hotel at 6 p.m. that evening. Driving my wife's new electric Volvo, I managed to arrive with five minutes to spare and complete the document of identity "issued in lieu of a passport" on the spot next door to Barefoot Bistro, which has a room that is essentially a deep freeze for vodka lovers complete with hooded parkas. Once again, it ended well. After a photo op, Jade was on her way.

ACKNOWLEDGEMENTS

AT CRITICAL TIMES in my life, many people gave me a lifeline that supported and inspired me to give more and move forward: Brian Aune, Deane Nesbitt, General Walt, Jacques Ménard, and John Cleghorn, to name a few. They were there in my life when I could have gone sideways.

My parents, of course, taught me to search for a better life and, above all, to become a good citizen. My mother spent her life giving to others, which is probably why God took her from us on Mother's Day. During the dark days of Vietnam, she was always there for me. She carried the burden of the unknown and never complained.

The US Marine Corps taught me to believe in myself, to never give up, and to really understand the meaning of "Semper fi"— always faithful—a sentiment that can be carried through life beyond the Marines. I'm grateful that at such a young age, the US Marines gave me responsibility over many young men of the finest fighting force in the world.

Sometimes people were not mentors but led by example as they entered my life. Like Ronna, my first wife, who I barely knew when I was shipped to Vietnam, but who wrote me hundreds of letters at a time when mail call was one of the few things I lived for; she was all about what she gave to me and my children, at a time we needed it most. My wife Chris has been a rock of support during some of the most difficult times. My daughters, Tasha and Krista, have been with me every step and always been the apple of my eye and a sounding board for me even when I may not have liked what they told me. And words cannot describe my gratitude to my personal assistant, Anne Ma, for over twenty-five years of service.

I'm also grateful to the large and historic institutions, like St. Paul's Hospital and Vancouver Public Library, that entrusted me with the responsibility of their treasured establishments at different times in my life. Dr. Julio Montaner of St. Paul's Hospital, who has been a friend of mine for thirty years, showed what it means to reach the highest level in your field and become a world leader in the treatment of HIV-AIDS. I am also grateful to the former executive director at St. Paul's Hospital Foundation, Linda Dickson, who inspired me to give more and enjoy it. At the Vancouver Public Library, I was blessed to know Paul Whitney, Sandra Singh, and Christina de Castell, chief librarians during my tenure, as well as board members Allan MacDougall, Lori Mathison, and, of course, Sally Warren, who recruited me in the first place. Brenda Van Engelen also supported me during the early years, and Jenny Marsh gave me relentless support in almost all ways during my tenure as chair.

This book wouldn't have been possible without the encouragement and support of Trena White of Page Two, my publisher, at a time during the Covid-19 pandemic when I really questioned why I was doing this. I am also indebted to Amanda Lewis and Scott Steedman, my editors at Page Two, who took the time to help me get the story on paper, as well as to Lida Lui, my other assistant, for her incredible support typing up what I dictated and researching dates and so on, in the midst of the pandemic, when I wrote the first three drafts over a long winter.

I've had the good fortune of having many good people in my life as friends, colleagues, employees, and fellow Marines; and people in so many charities I've been involved with, who believed that giving back was the right thing to do, and did it in a quiet way. This book is a testimony to the many people in my life who helped me along the way, although they may have never thought of it that way.

Giving back is what Tong Louie inspired me to do by simply not allowing me to quit, by saying, "You are just getting started, and don't be afraid to ask for money, and if you are turned down once, ask again."

Just try to do more with your life. If you get in a rut, try to get out. We all get in ruts. Try to move beyond them. Try to build something, however small it is, and give back. Constantly give back, but don't worry about giving back. And ask. I ask people all the time to give back. Ninety percent of them turn me down, but it's okay.

And be thankful. We live in an amazing country. We've got to go beyond the short-term problems we have, and we have many, and remember Canada's one of the best places in the world to live. We are fortunate to have the rule of law here, although it's being tested at the moment. Appreciate that, but don't be satisfied with the status quo. Push the limit.

INDEX

ABOUT THE AUTHOR

TERRY SALMAN, CM, BBM, is one of Canada's most dedicated philanthropists. Born in Montreal, he served as a sergeant with the US Marines during the Vietnam War before becoming a legend in mining finance. Terry was executive vice president of Nesbitt Thomson before leaving to form the financial firm Salman Partners, where he served as president, CEO, and co-director of research. Today, he is president and CEO of Salman Capital, chairman of New Pacific Metals, Chair Emeritus of the Vancouver Public Library Foundation, and Honorary Consul General of the Republic of Singapore. Terry holds a BA from Chaminade University of Honolulu, an MBA from the University of Hartford, and an honorary doctorate from the BC Institute of Technology. He received the Order of Canada in 2020 and the Public Service Star from the president of Singapore in 2021. The father of two grown daughters, Terry lives in West Vancouver with his wife, Chris.

ORIGINAL ORDERS

MEMORANDUM ENDORSEMENT on CG 3dMarDiv SO 220-65 of 25Aug65

From: Commanding Officer, MB USNB Pearl Harbor, Hawaii
To: Sgt Terry K. SAIMAN 2009444/0341 USMC

Subj: PCS Orders

1. You reported 8Feb66.

2. You are hereby assigned to ____ Brig Det MB Pearl ____ for duty.

J. A. BRABHAM
By direction